THE ART SCIENTIFIC

TWELVE ESSAYS

COLIN W. BELL

SPRING 2025

AN ART SCIENTIFIC
PRODUCTION

First Published in the UK July 2025

Revision: V.XI.MMXXV-I

https://artscientific.substack.com

https://colin.wigham.org/bell

Fifth Print

ISBN: 978-1-3999-6617-7

THE EDITOR'S PREFACE

TO

THE SPRING 2025 EDITION

I've been writing articles and essays, painting and looking at pictures my whole life. But like most things of that ilk, I've shut them away. I'm not sure why; it's just something I've always done. The grist to my mill wedded me to a life in technology—engineering, naval architecture, and computer science—where I developed an unlikely symbiotic view of the relationship connecting science with art. Perhaps the exactness of technological achievement instilled in me the idea that anything without peer review has limited worth, which, coupled with a natural shyness, sleepwalked me down a pathway to a state of conscious stalemate; I searched to find my art but stopped short of sharing it with the world. As Founder at *The Art Scientific*, I saw writing about art as an ambition reborn. But, like the business of technology that I was so eager to leave behind, I found the evolution to something better manifested itself as a familiar object lesson in two steps forward followed by one step backwards—perhaps that's always the way when reaching for the more rewarding goals in life.

Here at *The Art Scientific*, our mission is to present the history, theory, and science of art by blending analysis with memoir and anecdote to reveal fresh insights into the world we love: the world of art. From the Art of Painting in Renaissance Europe to the Art of the Digital; from chemistry, physics, and computer science to metaphysics and philosophy—it's all about *the art of science and the science of art*. A tall order, perhaps, but we invite our readers to share in this bright journey as we continue to travel hopefully.

There's a sobriety associated with technical preparations. It jars our swagger in the thick of the medium, and falters our immersion in the creative process. Painters love paint; it's our elixir, but when the painting's done, and the sobriety melds into the glow of satisfaction surrounding it, only then we can say it turned out well.

CONTENTS

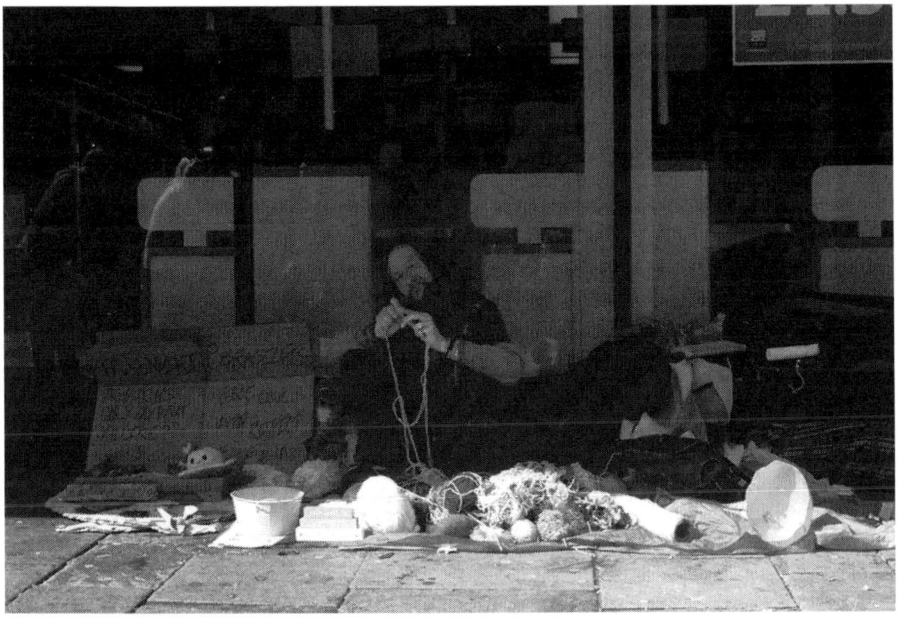

The Theory of NO BAD ART

To The Pure, All Things Are Pure

Oh no! They're at it again! Blurring boundaries! To clarify the passive voice here: *they*, are the purveyors of information, chiefly our news broadcasters and elected politicians. Blurring—the sort not requiring Photoshop—has become a very familiar trope in my world. In certain extreme cases, it can result in the terrible fatal pattern of distrust followed by hostility followed by conflict, like the conflated blur of nationhood with religion, which, for all the world, appear to me as entirely orthogonal constructs. If blurring is a deliberate attempt to obfuscate then, *they*, are a pernicious and manipulative sort with a scripted agenda hellbent on galvanising opinion around untruths; a brood of vipers. The alternative conclusion is *they* must be afflicted with such a severe case of fecklessness as to give a convincing impression of a brood of vipers. I appreciate that I've become more sensitive to blurring as I've grown older—arguably bordering on the pedantic. Political, religious, and scientific dogma, blurred or not, are intrusions into our lived experiences, but it's only from lived experiences that we assimilate what we believe to be true. Try writing something down you don't know! 'How far is Winnipeg from Montreal?' asked Richard Hannay in *The Thirty-Nine Steps*.

'Ah, a gentleman from Canada. You're welcome, sir. Winnipeg, the third city of Canada and the capital of the province of Manitoba. Distance from Montreal: 1,424 miles,' replied Mr. Memory.

We can all ask questions like that because they're deterministic; we recognise them as such, and we've learned to rely on someone like Mr. Memory to provide the answers.

When cosmologists observe how galaxies interact through gravity and measure the speed of stars at the outer edges of their orbits, they find significant discrepancies compared to predictions based on established laws of motion and universal gravitation. The forces that hold the universe together cannot be fully explained by classical physics derived from Sir Isaac Newton's seminal work, Philosophiæ Naturalis Principia Mathematica, which has served the scientific community admirably since 1687—the same physics that guided humans to the Moon and back. This shortfall led to the hypothesis that an invisible kind of matter must interact with gravity. It's estimated to account for more than five times the combined mass of everything we can see—including the very stuff we're made of, and all the billions of stars, dust, and gas in the universe. Its name is d*ark matter*.

In her primary school years, my daughter returned home one afternoon with a drawing she'd made. There was something intensely beguiling about it, I thought. How? There could be no story behind it—no compelling allegory hidden beneath the scribbled-on coloured pencil —forgive my churlishness perhaps—but after all, she was only six at the time! Had I reacted to a purely aesthetic impulse: the assertive economy of its outline, its harmonious colour balance, its striking composition, or perhaps some or all of those things? I pinned the drawing to the kitchen noticeboard, pondered my instinctive reaction a little deeper, and realised something else: to her, it was transient, discarded like an unloved doll! I eventually deduced that I'd affirmed guardianship over the little orphaned drawing by imagining a narrative for it of my own—my truth—and applied to it a value judgment usually reserved for my own work. Taking on the full measure of ownership had bridged the gap between what I'd felt and what I knew—it must have all happened instantaneously, I thought—like waking from a dream, convinced the dream is still unfolding. My daughter didn't reflect on modernism, post-Impressionism, nor any other 'ism' that might be encountered travelling back through time in the canon of the average art historian, nor did she tactically avoid the unfashionable. To the pure, all things are pure. She made her scribbles in a space where nothing existed before, a space where we feel only the eternal urge to record the wonder in which we find ourselves—like the daubers of prehistoric cave paintings who felt the raw compulsion to depict the world around them. There's no objective reason why my daughter's little drawing couldn't be elevated to the walls of a lofty show of post-twentieth century art —certainly the XL version of it—no forensic analysis needed, no tour guide description of its genre nor an absurd formulaic interpretation required. My emotive reaction revealed itself as an impulse to accept an imagined contract offered by the artist to the viewer. A backstory is always helpful in this respect, but each of us writes the contract. Some artists make it difficult for us; others, too easy—banal and cliché. Some spend their time arranging flowers.We resolve that artistic enlightenment—in all its rich intimacy, abstractness, and variability—can be reverse-engineered and embodied in a creation that triggers the desired responses. This is a complex challenge, given that our sensory signals are filtered through a consciousness shaped entirely by our uniquely individual lived experiences, and it would be irrational to assume that, for any two of us, these experiences would likely be the same.

In a protracted thought experiment, I resolved my own conflicts as a painter: I found that when the medium used in picture-making is laid bare and tangible, it reinforces the nature of handmadeness [made by human(s)] along with the essential hypothesis that *pictures are not images of something else but are themselves something*. As for the more general case, I'd argue that competency in reaching a manifestly rewarding outcome can be patently irrelevant. Opinions shall forever resolve themselves entirely as a matter of individual preference, where one's choices are guided by an indefatigable entity of consciousness—an entity that exists in the unknown, in the dark matter beneath the membrane of the human psyche.

Notwithstanding its successes in predicting the behaviour of inherently random systems—especially at atomic and subatomic levels where classical physics fails—quantum theory, when applied to explaining consciousness via the stochastic behaviour of neurons and neural activity, still leaves us in a tentative phase of understanding brain function and cognition as the building blocks of human consciousness. There are many things that one might find counterintuitive in the chronology of important discoveries in physics: that the heavier of Galileo Galilei's objects doesn't reach the ground before the lighter one when released simultaneously; that Sir Isaac Newton's object remains at constant velocity in the absence of some external force acting upon it; and outwith the luminiferous aether, in mathematics, that light, electricity, and magnetism, are one and the same thing; and that the progress of time is different for each of us in our life journey across Albert Einstein's space-time continuum. In a context where knowledge from one discovery informs decisions in the next, quantum mechanics is perhaps the last, best candidate to define consciousness. But if art speaks the natural language of consciousness, then words like *good*, *bad*, *better*, *worse*, *right*, or *wrong*, when used to measure it, amount to little more than narcissistic critique. The idea that *there can be no bad art*—only things one prefers over others—offers, by contrast, a universally applicable axiom for a theory that is both infinitely more edifying and, as some scientists might have it, classically counterintuitive.

Craft is the mastery over tools, materials, and techniques co-opted to make or nurture things to fulfil a required function—the how-to's. We play music, write prose, stretch canvas, mix paint, carve marble, orate speech, articulate motion, blow glass, form metal, and so on. For many, it's the element of craft that truly catalyses the alchemy in art. A runny wash in a watercolour painting, a fluffed line in a poem, or a flat note in a favourite tune are all discernible—we measure them against subliminal reference points: the standards we shape and refine through experience and learning. However, the dichotomy of such fallibility will always arise in the minds of artists who put their craft skills to use in an attempt to elicit an emotional human response on that basis. If a rule of good craft facilitating good art does exist, perhaps it can be measured by the inherently social phenomenon of popular consensus—which, some might argue, reflects the long-held belief in a set of universal rules governing the predictability of life on Earth, embodied in the laws of nature. The evolution of such laws has a three-billion-year head start on quantum mechanics; yet, while contemporary theories suggest an emerging science capable of describing the true nature of reality, they remain fragmented and lack the cohesion required for unification.

"How noble in reason, how infinite in faculty, In form and moving how express and admirable, In action how like an Angel, In apprehension how like a god, The beauty of the world, The paragon of animals ... And yet to me, what is this quintessence of dust?"

In this William Shakespeare monologue, Prince Hamlet reflects on the absoluteness of mortality in a way that might be perceived by an observer—in quantum terms, as one of an infinite number of possibilities—but, perhaps, any form of synthesis will always reach for an unattainable state of perfection, and we, the paragon of animals, shall always turn to the making of art—unpopular or not—in an attempt to convey the most compelling version of what it means to be human.

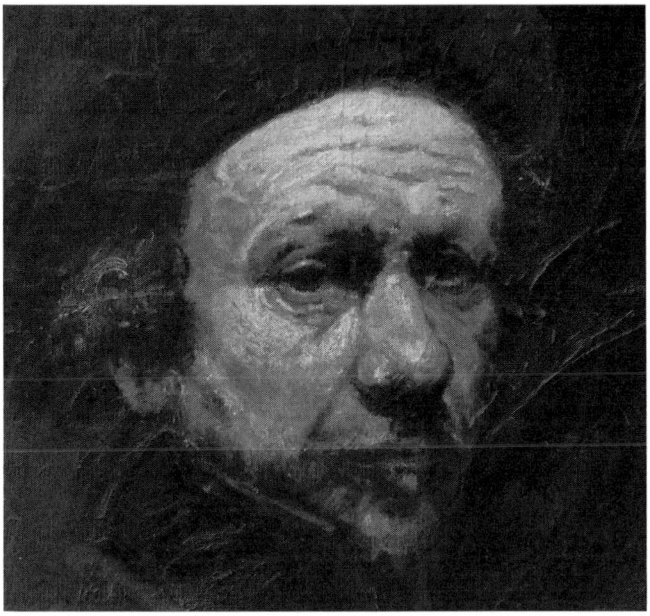

The Inner Workings of Rembrandt's Camera

The Great Photorealism Swindle

Have you ever heard the phrase The Art of Painting? It was used quite a bit back in the day—all the way back to the Italian Renaissance, as far as I can tell. I like to qualify the word *art* from time to time—it's a feeble attempt to preserve my sanity in the face of its misuse. The various incarnations of the phrase are far more meaningful to me than the solitary word *art*: the Art of Architecture, the Art of Dance, the Art of Gardening—whatever—they're all good, you see. The phrase The Art of Painting speaks to me of the box of tricks—supports, grounds, pigments, binding mediums, vehicles, and glazes—that can be deployed in a painter's hands for a single purpose. Put literally: to create an illusion of reality—whether realistic or imagined at some level of abstraction—by rendering a vision of that reality in light, colour, and form, onto a two-dimensional surface. Since time immemorial, this has been the painter's challenge. Imagine a scale on a graph representing a vision for a painted portrait, extending from the representational to the imaginary—from realism to abstract. Most of us would agree, I think, that a photographic portrait would typically provide a pretty compelling illusion of reality at the extreme representational end of the scale. It's no surprise, then, that portrait artists might welcome the powerful influence brought about by photography, and see great benefit in its impact on their workflow. From the letters of Vincent van Gogh,

"I am working on a portrait of Mother, because the black-and-white photograph annoys me so. Ah, what portraits could be made from nature with photography and painting! I always hope we will have a great revolution in portraiture."

Following the epoch of the Northern Renaissance—of Jan van Eyck and the portrait artists of Flanders—in Holland, a young Rembrandt's ambition was also firmly cast in the tradition of realism, primarily as a history painter, despite his highly recognisable attribution today as a portrait artist. In addition to his mastery of the techniques used in the application of paint in the medium of oil—of the effects of light, colour, and texture, particularly in the rendering of human flesh—he would've undoubtedly also been driven by aspects of comportment and the singular overarching objective of the commissioned portrait artist: to work within the finest margins possible of the imperative imposed by the genre—namely, the *likeness*. The phenomenon of likeness is quite extraordinary. Amidst the immeasurable minutiae of differences in the shape and juxtaposition of facial features—like a card trick, a sleight of hand scrying for traits of familiarity—we can assert a compelling likeness, even when refracted through a prism projecting an image more aptly measured nearer the imaginary end of our scale. It is this interplay between reality and imagination that shapes our understanding of identity and raises intriguing questions about the nature of recognition and the psychological mechanisms that inform our interpretation of the world.

I've often travelled to the National Gallery of Scotland to revisit a Rembrandt self-portrait—*Self-Portrait* [1657/1659], affectionately known to me as the Edinburgh Portrait. More often than not, I also find myself drawn to a detail in a different Rembrandt painting, usually hanging in the same room—a ten-centimetre-square patch of it, to be precise: *A Woman in Bed (Sarah Awaiting Tobias), Hendrickje Stoffels* [1643]. I invariably stand before it, pondering how the artist could be so casual in depicting an ostensibly smooth patch of skin with a scribble raising up the surrounding paint into ridges, like peaks on a furrowed field. I leave, always troubled by the same question: was this ungainly patch of paint accidentally left unfinished? I pause and ponder the thought—

'Snap out of it!' I then say—then console myself with the certainty that such a question is entirely irrational, perhaps even bordering on insanity. The passage of paint that so convincingly depicts Hendrickje's right forearm becomes strikingly clear when the painting is viewed from a distance: this is Rembrandt's calling card—his reminder that painting is just an illusion of reality, conjured from nothing but paint and the exuberant self-confidence in the technical ability of those who'd aspire to create it.

Upon examination of the Rembrandt oeuvre, we see a transition to his so-called rough manner of painting, which revealed itself most fully in the fifth decade of the seventeenth century. I'd argue that the seeds of his roughness were sown much earlier—as evidenced by less exaggerated examples of it in portraits he completed in his twenties—and that by his fifties, he had elevated his natural instinct for his painting technique into unbridled artistic performances: his impasto fuses into opaque patches modelled like liquid plastic; heightened luminosity rises through glazes; in the dark depths of shadow, there is form; in the mid-tones, glimpses of chromatic underpainting; and in the hues of his friendly palette, we find subtle and harmonious cohesion.

It's often quoted that when Rembrandt was approached with a question about why he painted so heavily and that his portraits could be picked up by the nose, he replied that he was no dyer but a painter. Rembrandt exploited the 'close-up' abstractness as a façade he masterfully manipulated to construct a convincing illusion of likeness and, within the same façade, transformed his sitters into portrayals of personality with staggering authenticity and allure. To many observers, Rembrandt's roughness creates a stronger illusion of reality, but this effect should not be interpreted as zealous spontaneity: his mastery was controlled, tempered by a set of rules which he refined to the highest degree of fidelity during numerous experiments painting his self-portrait. To reconcile the stir of excitement when Rembrandt requested an audience to reveal a finished portrait, and to be confronted by a negative reaction to his rough manner, would be challenging, to say the very least, if not to achieve a convincing likeness.

Remarkable facsimiles now appear as painted portraits in contemporary art concerned solely with the replication of photographic imagery—where every sinew seems strained to conceal the medium itself—a strong focus on alla prima—and where imitative photorealism is the clear and overriding imperative. To some, following in the light of Vincent's aspiration for a new, modern form of portraiture, this may not seem so wrong-headed—since the tendency to always look back in admiration of the old masters is no servant of progression. But given that both the Art of Photography and the Art of the Digital now exist as distinctly separate expansive forms of expression in their own right—each pursuing the selfsame illusion—it follows that the temptation to allow the blind replication of photographic imagery can only lead to a diminished form of artistry, with only the latent capacity to impress through admiration of the copyist's technical skill deployed in achieving it.

The discourse around Rembrandt's artistry is, quite inevitably, reduced to a discussion of technique—albeit one that has grafted useful theories onto the topic over the years, some expressed with such exuberance and aplomb that others have described them as bordering on myth. From a practitioner's point of view, the picture is complicated: the degree to which Rembrandt's paint and glazes have altered over time is unknowable, and comparative observations are hampered when familiarity with the medium reflects modern practice, where oil paint, with its modern formulations for pigment and binding mediums, is taken straight from tubes. Certainly, the plasticity observed in Rembrandt's upper (foreground) layers—appropriated in his whites—suggests the use of viscous binding components, and scientific examination reveals his method of working from background to foreground, incorporating a monochromatic underpainting and a selective use of imprimatura, as part of his workflow.

The mobility within his paint layers—about which we can universally eulogise—is the result of the unique combination of filters he seemed able to attach to his camera's lens, long before cameras were invented. If we were to travel back in time and gift a smartphone camera to the old masters of realism, I'd be curious to know whether they'd feel threatened by such an unsaintly miracle of technology. I suspect not in the case of Rembrandt! If talent is the best assurance of success, then it's no surprise that fear, to some, might look so like joy to others.

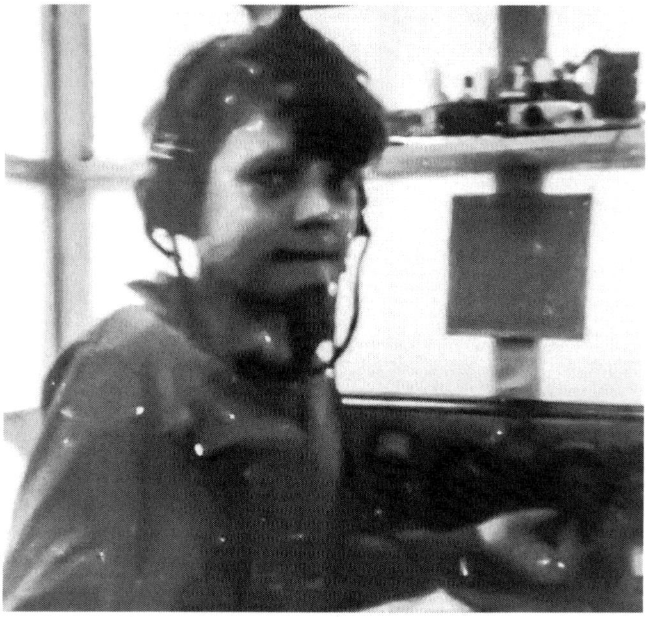

The Enigma of Yellow

The Rainbow World of Miniature Planetary Systems

'Yellow belly custard green snot pie, all mixed together with a dead dog's eye. Mix it, mix it, mix it thick, then drink it down with a hot cupa sick.'

Such is one recollection of the din of playtime banter at Addison Potter School for Infants. I was less inclined to chant that rhyme out loud but rather digest the little gruesome confection—not literally, of course—but wonder: yellow; if I were to paint that belly, what kind of pigment would I use, and from where would it come? Following graduation to the big school, Mr. Trovorrow, our headmaster, explained that Indian Yellow was a pigment produced by boiling the urine of cows fed only on a diet of mango leaves and that the method had been abandoned due to the unethical treatment of the beasts coerced in the making of it. Might we embellish our rhyme with a new crudity by liking piss to custard for our vile consumption, we joked? I chose not to dwell on the green ingredient amidst the madding rush of can-kicking *cockurouso*—there was quite enough hockle about—but what of the mixing that makes it thick? Later, breaking eggs for the baking of a Victoria sponge during one of our more raucous and unruly lessons, dubbed 'Domestic Science', we whispered whether there might be some elusive emulsifying agent lurking undiscovered somewhere in our recipe. But I found myself immersed in a defiantly silent contemplation, transfixed by a different challenge—the more pressing scientific conundrum associated with the mango leaf story: what is yellow, anyway?

'Is custard made from pee?' I joked with a classmate.

'Probably—these egg yolks came out of hens' arses,' came the reply.

The teacher intervened: 'It's a scary thought that colour doesn't actually exist in our world; there's only radiation coming from the sun. We can only see certain rays of it. We call it the visible spectrum because we have receptors in our eyes that are sensitive to them. These send signals to the brain, which creates the thing we call colour. It's all an illusion, really!'

I interjected, 'Imagine a world without colour!'

'But there is such a world—for creatures unlike us!'

'How does colour get into things?' I asked.

The teacher faltered. 'It doesn't. It only comes out of things! Rays within the visible spectrum are absorbed differently by different materials—they're eaten up, if you like—and the leftovers are reflected back at us. Those are the ones we see.'

'If they're eaten, why doesn't everything just get fatter and fatter?' laughed the classmate.

'Well, that's a question about energy. We'd need a conversation with Mr Einstein about that. But before you scoff,' said the teacher, 'not all yellow things are made of the same stuff—custard isn't a bit like urine'

We're taught that, along with red and blue, yellow *is* a colour that can't be created by mixing other pigments of different hues together. The assertion that yellow is described as a primary colour, led me to my uncanny fallacy: that this same principle also applies to the spectrum of coloured light, too. But, we're told that yellow is produced as a secondary colour by combining red and green rays in the coloured light model where, red is considered a primary along with green and blue.

Albert Einstein, in his Introduction to the 1931 reprint of Isaac Newton's Optiks or *A Treatise of the Reflections, Refractions, Inflections and Colours of Light*, first published in 1704, wrote,

"The conceptions which he used to reduce the material of experience to order seemed to flow spontaneously from experience itself, from the beautiful experiments which he ranged in order like playthings and describes with an affectionate wealth of detail. In one person he combined the experimenter, the theorist, the mechanic-and, not least, the artist in exposition. He stands before us strong, certain, and alone: his joy in creation and his minute precision are evident in every word and in every figure."

Einstein clearly respected the innovations described in Optiks, chiefly among them, the spectral composition of light and the elementary theory of the rainbow; all universally recognised as the foundation of colour theory. In Optiks, Isaac Newton queried,

"Do not several sorts of Rays make Vibrations of several bignesses, which according to their bignesses excite Sensations of several Colours, much after the manner that the Vibrations of the Air, according to their several bignesses excite Sensations of several Sounds? And particularly do not the most refrangible Rays excite the shortest Vibrations for making a Sensation of deep violet, the least refrangible the largest for making a Sensation of deep red, and the several intermediate sorts of Rays, Vibrations of several intermediate bignesses to make Sensations of the several intermediate Colours?"

There is a constant that exists in the evolution of human kind. It's the same constant that first lit a fire, first made bread from cultivated fields of seed, invented prime movers, and conjured up electricity from the most obfuscated properties of the earth. No mechanism can substitute genius—there have been precious few among us like Sir Isaac Newton—but this same constant pervades the great unseen, the mundane practical, the empiricisms that improve our knowledge of the world at each tiny iteration of our evolution. It's been known by artists for centuries that a limited palette consisting of a small set of pigments can mix a diverse gamut of colours. In the tricks we painters play, we see green as a secondary colour on the palette: a mixture of Naples Yellow or Yellow Ochre with Ultramarine or Azurite can make a greenish hue. No raw pigment found on earth produces a pure colour effect as idealised in the coloured light model: vermilion, from cinnabar, is orangish-red; red ochre, from hematite, is brownish-red. Equally, artists' colours within each primary band of red, yellow, and blue available to buy in tubes are nuanced. Any mixture produces a less saturated colour than their counterparts in the form of raw pigment—contrast, if you will, the beautiful vivid and memorable green, from verdigris, seen in Jan van Eyck's Arnolfini with any green that can be made on the palette.

To explain the phenomena of reflection and refraction, Sir Isaac Newton famously posits in Optiks that light is fundamentally composed of particles—he called them "corpuscles"—and his theory remained unchallenged for over one hundred years until the corpuscular was debunked by the scientific community in the early part of the nineteenth century purporting overwhelming evidence (including the double-slit experiment) to validate the competing theory that describes light as a waveform. Paradoxically, Optiks also contains observations and "queries" that concur with the idea of light travelling as a wave. Newton's endearing term *bigness*, is an analog of wavelength when taken as an energy impulse riding on the crest of a wave which, Newton observed, when refracted through a prism is separated into the composite frequencies corresponding to the colours of the rainbow. The concept of the "quanta" emerged in 1905 when Albert Einstein proposed that light consists of discrete energy packets, later named photons, to explain his so-called photoelectric effect and Newton's observation that a particle indeed does exist as a constituent of light was broadly acknowledged in wave-particle duality theory as a fundamental aspect of the new science of quantum mechanics: that particles, like electrons and photons, can exhibit both wave-like and particle-like behaviours.

In a new Preface for the 1931 reprint of Optiks, I. Bernard Cohen alludes to the superposition of ideas,

"Every age finds a particular sympathy for certain masterpieces of science and of art. Our present age lends a particularly appreciative eye and ear to the paintings of Lucas Cranach the elder and Jheronimus Bosch, and the poetry of John Donne and William Blake. Since our reading in the past great works of science is conditioned by the science of our own time, our interpretations and evaluations are as different from those of the last century as our tastes in poetry and art."

The mixing of coloured light and the blending of pigments within a binding medium to make paint are processes delineated in science as *additive* and *subtractive* respectively. These are abstract models in that the exact balance of primary colours has been adapted as best fit for use in modern digital display technology and for printing using ink. They each have their role in creating the illusion of colour, as do we painters.

In *The Science of Painting* (1891), Jean-George Vibert, wrote,

"Then, they must be told also that there were magicians called Veronese, Rubens, Delacroix, and many others, who knew more about colouring than any scientist in the world ; for with their colours they have created a language which speaks to

the soul, which communicates feeling and life, long before science has even suspected that coloured rays influenced the brain."

Returning to my schoolboy grapple with colour theory: paint is matter and light's perpetual interaction with all matter causes a resonance to occur and, in response, various frequencies are emitted as a distribution of energy in the frequency domain existing between the observed and the observer. The physics is absolute but the vagueness is human: I accept that the additive model produces the purist colour sensation possible and that the cones and rods within the cellular structure of the retina and the metaphysical also play a part, but when I mix cinnabar (reddish) with malachite (greenish) on the palette, it very predictably produces a brown hue (somewhere between that of the natural earth pigments of raw umber and burnt sienna) because the rays absorbed by each constituent hue in the mixture are still absorbed causing the resultant hue to become less bright; each pigment retains its distinctness in respect to its capacity to absorb photons. Vincent van Gogh's sunflowers appeared to me a duller brown in the relatively low ambient energy intensive conditions of a darkened room; the subtleties within the perfect flesh tones of my portrait painted under the warm light of a filament bulb were all but destroyed when seen in the full sun of the morning. As for my yellow enigma: the effect of a material absorbing light from the spectrum, allowing a range between red and green frequencies to be emitted is to combine to make a colour we humans might concur is yellow.

In an attempt to invent a renewed parody of colour—photons being batted about amongst clouds of electrons by millions of tiny pinball flippers in a state of perpetual excitement, perhaps—I realise still that the theory doesn't transcend the prosaic bleakness of science speak; our Yellow Belly Custard skit is perfect the way it is: of its time, and of its place!

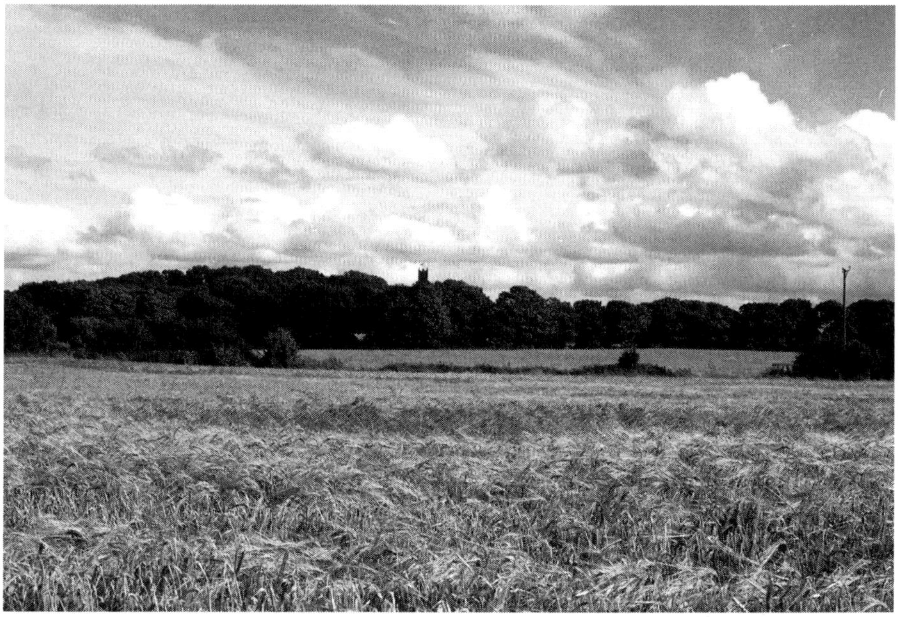

What Lies Beneath

The Not So Common Ground for Painters

There are things in life seldom more satisfying to me than confronting a freshly prepared ground for painting. Theatrically mounted centre-stage, clean and steadfast in form, and rewarding in its hand-made aspect. With nothing left to chance, a swell of exited anticipation stirs in the knowledge that those first daubs mark the beginning of a new journey in picture making.

I'm not afraid of the ninja art thief—the one who'd abseil from the skylight of a smart gallery, deftly evade the laser infrared beams of the intruder alarm system in the dead of night, to make off with my masterpiece; its canvas assuredly rolled up underarm, having separated it from its frame with a knife. It's just I see little merit these days in using canvas as a support for paint, that's all! I do, of course, gravitate toward the tradition of canvas. I love to catch the aroma of it freshly unfurled from its roll, like the intoxicating waft of greenhouse tomatoes in the summer garden air. But, I gird my loins. The prospect of disguising its warp and weft with a layer of ground applied thickly enough to avoid its texture imparting its vexing regularity on the resulting surface appearance of my pictures is, for me, always an unwanted chore. Let's face it, the pattern of canvas weave left visible through the painting as a right of passage of the painters' craft—worn like a badge of merit, some may say —is all very twee!

The stem of the flax plant: retted, combed, and spun; woven into precious linen cloth, was shipped by caravan and boats rigged in canvas sail and braided yarn along the fertile crescent of the Tigris and Euphrates rivers for the adornment of the dynastic rulers harking back to the Pharaohs of ancient Egypt. The beguiling vision of flowers cultivated in vast swathes of shimmering pale blue fields might pervade the image of ancient Mesopotamia, where the plant was indigenous. But, the great significance of canvas introduced into European painting practice emerged much later—from the fifteenth century onwards—when Venice had evolved as a busy trading hub connecting Europe with the Middle East and Asia, reaching its zenith by the height of fame accorded to them by the masters of the Venetian school.

Giorgio Vasari, writes of the early adoption of canvas by Margaritone [Margarito] da Arezzo [c. 1250-1290], in respect to averting common problems with supports for paint made from planks of wood,

"From what is seen in his works, as regards painting, he was the first who considered what a man must do when he works on panels of wood, to the end that they may stay firm in the joinings, and that they may not show fissures and cracks opening out after they have been painted; for he was used to put over the whole surface of the panels a canvas of linen cloth, attached with a strong glue made from shreds of parchment and boiled over a fire; and then over the said canvas he spread gesso, as is seen in many panels by him and by others."

In the *Life of the Giovanni Bellini*, Vasari also describes the Venetian custom of painting on stretched canvas in place of wooden panels. In Cennino Cennini's treatise *Il libro dell' Arte o Trattato della Pittura*, written at the turn of the fifteenth century, in *Of the way to work on linen or hempen cloth*, Cennini provides instruction for stretching canvas over a frame which, by association, relates the term canvas with textile fabric woven from hemp,

"Now let us speak of the way to work on cloth, that is, either linen or canvas, and you will observe this method in painting on any kind of cloth; that in the first place it is necessary to stretch it firmly on the frame (stretcher), nailing the seams straight first, then going round and round with little nails, spreading it equally and in an exact manner, getting all the threads precisely in the right direction."

Still, as much as a generation later in Rome, Raphael's Transfiguration was executed on a three inch thick composite panel made of joined planks of wood and the use of wooden panels persisted in the Low Countries until the time of Rembrandt. The notion of using textile fabrics stretched over frames as a support for paint must have appeared as an entirely incongruous proposition to Raphael and his contemporaries plying their trade during the Renaissance in Italy when tempera and oil bindings mixed with pigments to make paint had long been laid on wooden panels. Notwithstanding the disadvantage of the hygroscopic tendency of fabrics (the propensity to draw moisture from the atmosphere), canvas, not manufactured specifically as a support for paint, but for general purpose use such as sailcloth, grew in popularity amongst the artistic community due to its lightness and flexibility. Vasari also writes of the convenience of canvas, which,

"...when rolled up is of easy transport."

The latin *cannapaceus* "made of hemp" from which the word canvas is derived, provides early testament to the practice of using hemp—extracted from the stem of the Cannabis plant indigenous to Asia—in the manufacture of artefacts designed for rough handling duties like rope and loosely woven textile fabric sacks, due to the relatively high tensile strength of its long fibres which, although not specifically manufactured as a support for paint, found its way into the hands of painters for that purpose. Following in the wake of confidence the Venetians had acquired in the craft of developing grounds for paint laid on canvas—reaching its technological zenith in the colossus that is Tinterento's *Il Paradiso* [22m x 9m] at the Doge's Palace—the Florentine Sandro Botticelli's *The Birth of Venus*, provides us with perhaps one of the best-known, relatively early large-scale work, painted on canvas. Fast-forward to the end of the transition from wood to canvas: Caravaggio's famous altar pieces are very substantive objects made of surprisingly coarse plain-weave hemp, and the portability of such large paintings presented tangible challenges in their own right. Not so in the case of easel paintings: the celluloid depiction of Vincent van Gogh's flimsy canvas flailing about like a kite in the Mistral around the fields of Arles, is a far cry from the marble halls of Caravaggio's Rome and the studios turning out epically proportioned history scenes throughout the seventeenth and eighteenth centuries. The discourse amongst the French Impressionists—the pre-eminent movement in Europe near the end of the nineteenth century—focussed more on the type of weave and thread count than of the plant genus, but the preceding two hundred years saw the soft smooth surface of machine woven linen steadily appear as the material of choice in artists' supplies, and was thoroughly established as the de facto within the custom and practice of their time.

In the wake of a remarkable string of technological innovations beginning with the cotton gin and culminating with the development of the steam-powered loom, and when toilers of the world toiled under the yoke of the Industrial Revolution, the textile industry evolved a highly sophisticated mechanised process for the mass production of cloth from cotton. From plant to cloth, the production of linen became inherently more protracted and expensive than cotton production, and the viability of linen put to its traditional uses within the global textile economy gradually declined as cotton fabrics became more readily affordable to the market. The incursion of cotton for mass consumption as a general-purpose fabric occurred before the turn of the twentieth century. Within a similar timeframe, the supply of Jute—a rough natural fibre from the Corchorus genus—into Europe via the trade routes established with the Indian subcontinent, was manufactured as hessian (or burlap) which provided a cheap and more sustainable alternative to hemp canvas as a coarsely woven support.

In modern convention, a *ground* for painting is a preparation of a so-called *size* and a *primer* applied to the support in various coatings. This loosely corresponds to Vasari's summary of Margaritone da Arezzo's practice: his parchment, boiled down with the fat removed, produces the gelatinous adhesive referred to as *size*; his gesso acting as a primer. The essential requirement of a ground is to obviate the damaging effects that would occur in appearance and to the integrity of the substrate if paint were to be applied to the support directly. The ground also helps create a smooth and even surface to take the paint layer and, at the same time, prevent paint from being absorbed into the surface, such that it can stand-up of its own accord. Before the advent of precision machinery, when larger wooden panels were, by necessity, constructed from individual boards, the ground would also serve as a filler used to conceal the seams formed by the abutment of one board against the other, as well as the general undulations present in the surface when primitive hand tools developed for woodcutting were all that was available. Cennini's ground corresponds to fifteenth century Italian where a primer of Plaster of Paris was applied in layers and scraped smooth over three or four coats of size applied hot and allowed to dry between each coating. Interestingly, Jehan-George Vibert, writing in 1892 in his *The Science of Painting*, describes his ground as a paste incorporating the properties of both a size and a primer, which he describes as sizing. The ground can take a myriad of forms: Vibert comically cites ingredients of oysters' shells, crabs' eyes, stags' horns, pigs' blood, fishes' bladders, cows' tails, sheep's feet, and powdered insects, but favoured caseine described as cheese paste (commercial grade, as opposed to crust of Gruyère) with the addition of the pigment Zinc White whereas Cennini's Plaster of Paris is essentially gesso: a substance made from gypsum (sulphate of lime) according to his recipe, but can also contain chalk (calcium carbonate). Both Vibert's paste and Cennini's Plaster of Paris contain an amount of size similar to the aforementioned in different proportions to act as the binding agent.

I've never questioned the plethora of advice available regarding the importance of the sizing procedure. It's too important to ignore. So much so, I also apply size to wooden panels in preparation for paint on the assumption that an adhesive layer would reinforce the sticking power of the ground which is another important characteristic of the size when protecting the delicate fibres of a canvas substrate. There are a number of traditions that earn a certain swagger in my studio; forays into the ancient crafts unimagined by the untrained eye. Stirring a pungent liquor in a kettle bubbling over a stove, like a prop in an alchemist's workshop scene, can provoke much amusement for the unsuspecting onlooker. The making of a glue for use as a sizing agent is one such tradition. I purchase rabbit skin from a supplier pre-prepared in granule form. The granules, or pellets, can be soaked overnight for rehydration, then immersed and heated in a proportion of water, stirring until the mixture assumes a viscosity such that when cooled to tepid, it forms a thick jelly-like consistency. After testing for the correct gloopiness, the mixture can be reheated and reconstituted as necessary to make the mixture more or less diluted as required to arrive at the final result. The size should be applied to the support with a fully charged brush by adopting a pouncing or stippling action in the case of canvas when the glue is still warm. Max Doerner, in his *The Materials of the Artist and their use in Painting* [1962] asserts that body pigments need to be added to primings (grounding preparation) to improve covering power and to avert considerable colour degradation when in direct contact with oil. His tenet suggests a white ground is the overarching requirement in that layers of transparent coloured glazes subsequently applied can leverage a high degree of luminosity from its underlying brightness. White grounds provide optical clarity when transferring a traced sketch or cartoon however, should the plan be to apply brighter hues opaquely [consider the work of Rembrandt], then the coloured ground can be made a key element in influencing the envisaged tonal composition of the final artwork, moreover, the workflow preferred in achieving it. I've yet to avail myself of the pleasure of making paste from cheese; I've been known to start with gypsum and whiting but avoid like the plague anything commercially available in tins containing synthetic resin (acrylic) and normally supplement with dry pigment of one hue or another to add colour to the ground.

Linen is less abrasive than cotton, smoother, more durable, and less moisture retentive. The common pre-stretched, pre-primed shop-bought canvases generally available in the shops are a pitfall to any budding artist and something I take great pain to avoid. They're invariably woven from cotton. I've winced at the sight of a sturdy hog-hair brush eroded to an unhappy stump using this kind of product. I can only guess at the composition of the primer used with economy in mind; in larger sizes, their porous wooden stretchers, devoid of any heartwood, have a propensity to warp. I cringe at the sight of low carbon steel staples—as spiky as Caravaggio's artichokes—minded as I am of their vulnerability to corrosion having left them out in a damp studio for long periods between sessions. In the case of easel painting, modern laminated wooden panels are superior to this class of product; panels and boards are generally manufactured to a high degree of precision and, when properly seasoned and dried, offer a highly durable support for paint. The use of natural wood also avails we painters of certain bragging rights; as they say: "if it was good enough for Rembrandt...!"

There's a sobriety associated with technical preparations. It jars our swagger in the thick of the medium, and falters our immersion in the creative process. Painters love paint; it's our elixir, but when the painting's done, and the sobriety melds into the glow of satisfaction surrounding it, only then we can say it turned out well.

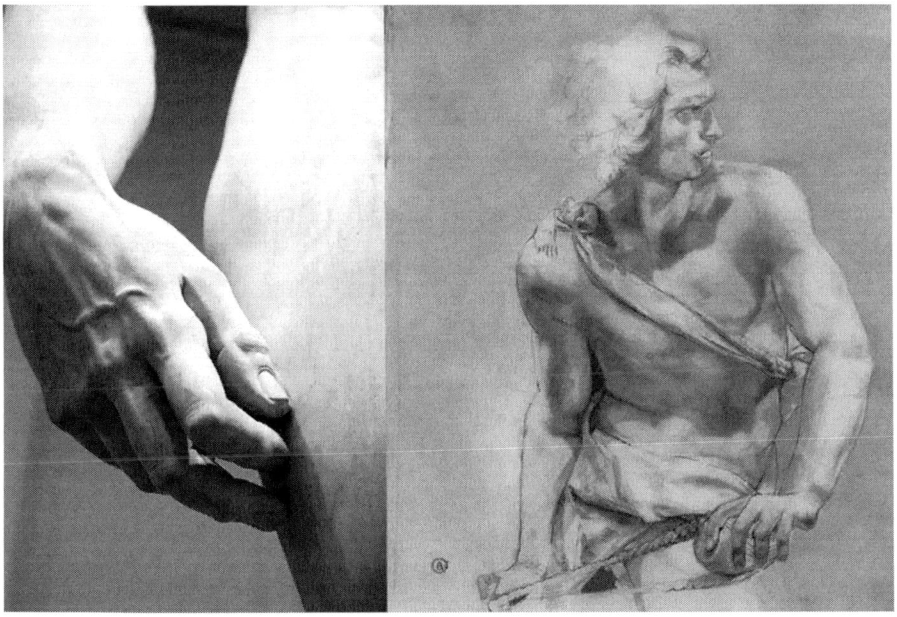

David *'ad'* David

Michelangelo • Bernini • Renaissance to Baroque

The early Renaissance in Western Europe saw the first flush of realism in the Art of Painting when the Christian clergy preached the teachings of the church—all about god and the miraculous lives of the saints -to a largely illiterate society. Realism in Renaissance Europe was all about making the miraculous appear real. This requirement played an essential role in the development of the visual arts, especially in Italy, calling upon the feuding factions of provincial mercantile dynasties and the incumbents in the higher echelons of the papacy, and their incomparable wealth, to be courted for patronage during this period. The route to Michelangelo Buonarroti's legacy was driven by his devout faith. His art was emblematic of the constraints imposed upon him by the orthodoxy of his beliefs, including that his talent was bestowed upon him by god himself. He would be exalted by the mastery of his craft reborn in the ancient grandeur of monumental art. He resolved that '*No one shall genuflect before a Madonna only to discover later that it was the fishmonger's daughter.*'; that the Madonna shall be depicted both as a mother and as a virgin; that the child Christ shall appear not as an infant without wisdom.

Gian Lorenzo Bernini was a prodigy of a different sort. His art was sponsored by the counter-reformation agenda of the Catholic church with the ambition of imbuing deity with the heightened drama of emboldened realism.

By the early seventeenth century, the chains tethering them to the Bonfire of the Vanities had long been severed, the controlling authority subverted, and the revolt against Martin Luther '*...and all this sink of Roman sodomy that ceaselessly corrupts the church of God*', led to the expansive transformation in art known as the Baroque. Both the Davids engage with their immediate space threatened by an invisible enemy. In Michelangelo's David we see the idealised gaze of confident resolve and a posture of comparable confidence in strength—marble made monument. In Bernini's David, we see '*the powerful knitted brows,*' and, '*the terrible fixity of the eyes,*' in swift ardour of action and athleticism made in his own likeness—marble made flesh.

Such was the transformation from the Renaissance to the Baroque—a call to arms by the dilettante to those emerging as the new aesthetes, the new bringers of truth.

The path he carved was not of stone alone,
But faith—unyielding—his guiding force.
Michelangelo, by holy whispers known,
Believed his gift was born of sacred name.
A servant to the doctrine he embraced,
His chisel guided by God's spoken law.
And through his mortal hands, the world was graced,
By truths divine that held the world in awe.
His forms ideal, with beauty stretched to hide:
The David—youthful flesh with manly hands,
A god made man, or giant boy on heaven's side—
Held firm before the world's unyielding foe.
His angel thugs, tangled, wildly fly,
Serpents curled with sin fall in judgment's fire.
Moses horned, his rule in pensive thought,
And Mary masked in youthful face, yet rapt
In rebirth sought.
Bernini, born of nature, not creed,
Felt marble pulse with love's wounds unhealed.
A different prayer, where flesh and spirit bleed
In ecstasies forbade his stone revealed—
Teresa, pierced by passion's spear,
A soul undone beneath the sculptor's sin.
His David in sinew and flesh and swing,
Coiled tension yields to his mighty sling.
Where one found God in discipline,
The other ached of flesh and skin.
Two hearts, two souls, through time's enduring gaze.
Both saints of stone, yet carved from different realms within.

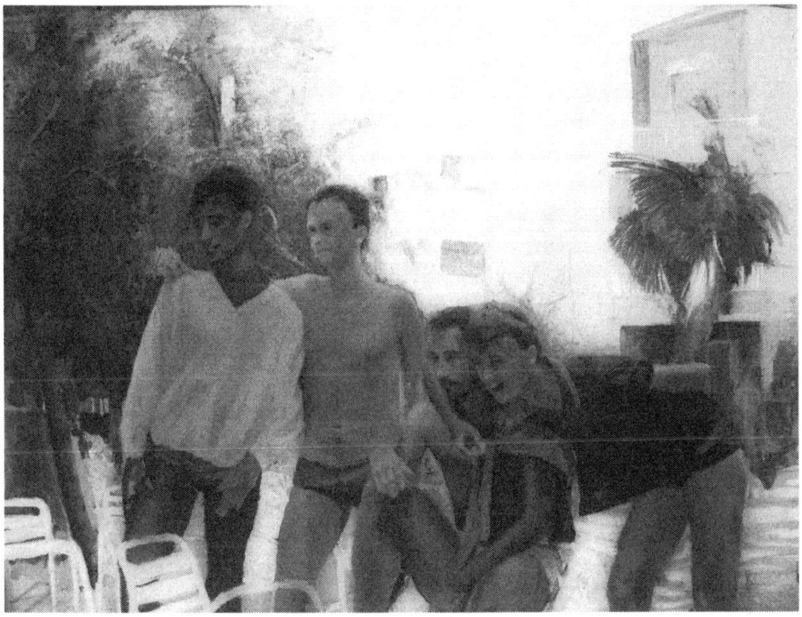

The Arrow of Time

Rites of Passage

Entropy describes the direction of natural processes. It's a measure of disorder: the greater the number of ways a system can be arranged, the higher its entropy. As the universe expands, the number of possible arrangements for matter and energy increases—meaning the universe has more entropy today than it had yesterday. In this sense, the future is more disordered than the past.

We typically think of time as flowing in a single direction, continuously turning the future into the past. This is known as time's arrow—the asymmetric direction of time that drives the evolution of the universe. But there's another way to think about time: by focusing on how things change rather than on the ticking clock. Things are always changing; always in the direction of increasing entropy. When events occur, the total energy of a system is redistributed in such a way as to maximise the number of possible arrangements. That's what gives rise to *cause and effect*: a consequence of the universe's tendency toward greater disorder. It's far less likely to evolve toward a more ordered state—such as that which existed in the past. We can't go back; we can't unscramble eggs—no matter how much we long to revisit history in a mission to set the record straight.

Homage or not Homage

I travelled to London from Newcastle on the cheapest bus ticket known to humanity to see a Rembrandt self-portrait. None of my peers could have cared less—though, thinking back, I may have rudely avoided sharing the idea with them anyway—but climbing aboard the bus at that lonely hour felt, for the most part, like an empty challenge. It's been more than forty years since I welled with tears at the National Gallery. I looked again at my old friend yesterday (*Self Portrait* 1640) and read along with a virtual spokesperson's commentary,

'This is one of dozens of self portraits by Rembrandt. We see the artist in confident pose, self assured, dressed in expensive looking fur and velvet, his hat laced with jewels. But, though he is a Dutchman living in the sixteen-forties, Rembrandt is wearing the clothes of a gentleman of the fifteen-twenties and his pose is based on paintings by Dürer, Titian and Raphael from a similar date. So, as the subject of the painting, Rembrandt is portraying himself as a Renaissance gentleman, and as the artist he is both paying homage to and directly comparing himself with the most famous artists of that time.'

..."confident pose"; "expensive looking." To whom does he appear confident? To whom does his apparel seem expensive? If the claim is that Rembrandt's clothing in this portrait reflects early sixteenth-century Italian fashion, then he must have had a lifelong obsession with retro—he's dressed similarly in many of his self-portraits right up to 1669: a tabbaard, doublet, pinafore, smock, and shirt. And as for flamboyant headgear, *The Night Watch* suggests that seventeenth-century Amsterdam was the epitome of extravagant flamboyancy in the art of millinery. I pondered this for a few minutes more until my bafflement returned in the form of an audible exhale of frustration. Never mind the low opinion of his fashion sense—why should Rembrandt's use of a simple compositional device convince us that he deliberately set out to pay homage in a gesture of deference? What an absurd supposition! What kind of narrative could accommodate such a distortion? I wondered,

'...it's to be displayed alongside self portraits by young people who have considered how they would like to be seen by their peers, when, like Rembrandt, they reach the age of thirty four.'

My thoughts spiralled inwardly into sarcasm: so when these youngsters reach thirty-four, should they also hope to be compared with someone who lived a hundred years earlier? Is that really the full measure of ambition we offer young artists setting out to change the world? No. No—and we ought not to assume the same of Rembrandt. The compositional device here refers to a curious conversation piece in art history. It stems from the placement of a ledge (or sill) between the sitter and the viewer to provide a natural frame for a half-body portrait. Rembrandt saw this in Raphael's portrait of Baldassare Castiglione and Titian's *A Man with a Quilted Sleeve* in collections in Amsterdam. There's a rare note in Rembrandt's hand, scribbled around a crude little sketch he made of the Raphael portrait. Framed in ink, the note translates as,

Count Balthasar de Castiglione by Raphael, sold for 3500 guilder. The entire shipment fetched 59,456 guilders at Luke van Nuffelen. Anno 1639.

A gentleman called Alphonso Lopez, a dealer known to have owned a significant collection of paintings housed in Amsterdam at that time, bid at the auction to buy the painting by Raphael for the considerable sum worthy of special note on Rembrandt's sketch. Lopez's collection also included the Titian portrait.

The two self-portraits by Rembrandt in question are the etching *Self-Portrait leaning on a stone sill* of 1639 and his painted portrait *Self-Portrait 1640*. There's a strong correlation between the rate of output of commissioned portraits by Rembrandt and downturns in his financial affairs—including the period leading up to his eventual bankruptcy. His well-to-do patrons, riding high on the hubris of the Dutch Golden Age, provided a handsome income stream that supported both his vocation as a history painter and his passion as an avid collector of antiquities and fine art. Might Rembrandt, noting the monetary value attached to the Raphael portrait (as recorded in his sketch), have seen an opportunity for self-promotion by executing *Self-Portrait* (1640) as a showpiece of his skills as a portrait artist? Certainly, the self-portraits that bracket 1639–1640—each taken from his right-hand side, with raised-hand posture —display less subtlety and refinement than the 1640 portrait, leaning more toward his natural, expressive manner evident throughout his oeuvre. With self-promotion in mind, might he depict himself in a guise that might appeal to his would-be clients enamoured with Titian and the elevated repute of the Venetian School? Might he inscribe the word *Conterfeycel* below his signature on the painting which translates from old Dutch as *Portrait* or *Portraiture?* Might he fashion the painting with a curved top to make of itself a decorative adornment worthy of the grand houses of Amsterdam? Might he make prints (potentially in large numbers) from etchings as a collateral part of this same self-promotion?

Well, yes, yes, yes, yes and, yes.

I'd ask you to challenge the flirtatious hyperbole that invariably gushes forth in a cloud of coddled words when art historians describe important figures in art such as Rembrandt. He plied his trade, as would any merchant, to make his living using brushes and paints in seventeenth-century Amsterdam. In this *plain* version of the truth, the *Self-Portrait 1640* is neither deferential nor a homage. He was not infallible. To my eye, the etching lacks strength in its contrasts and shadow; the foreshortening of the arm to the elbow, compounded by the billowing sleeve, makes the head appear enlarged. The proportions here compare poorly to the graceful posture depicted in the painted portrait. As for the broader comparisons with Titian: Rembrandt never travelled to Italy, and so it is unlikely he was ever fully acquainted with the formula attributed to Titian when shaping his own portraiture tradition. It was *Self-Portrait at the Age of 63*, not *Self-Portrait* 1640, that moved me to tears back in the eighties. I could, of course, eulogise about that moment, wrap it in a cloud of coddled words and press my truth upon others, but suffice it to say, in bidding a fond farewell in the year of his passing, Rembrandt left us an enduring lesson in the art of the painted portrait that, even today, remains stubbornly impossible to surpass.

We All Lived in a Little Yellow House

We've all heard John, Paul, George, and Ringo reflect on their favourite Beatles songs. There's something precious about the authenticity of those subjective responses—that's what we love. It's about art, after all, straight from the mouths of those who made it. We're immeasurably lucky to live in the age of television. It's the intimacy of TV that captivates us when intimacy is on display. The world I watched fill up with cathode ray tubes, electron guns, and phosphorescent screens brought Modernism—including Beatlemania—

into every home on the planet. Andy Warhol's full fifteen minutes of fame famously eluded Vincent van Gogh during his lifetime, but he gave us something better—something far better: he wrote letters. Lots of letters. *The Complete Letters of Vincent Van Gogh* is a remarkable text from one of the pre-eminent authors of Modernism; his impressive intellect, his sufferings, his unerring dedication to his art; ebullience and honesty flow from the pen of a man better known to us today for his brush.

"...I am hard at it...the painting of some big sunflowers ... If I carry out this idea there will be a dozen panels, so the whole thing shall be a symphony in blue and yellow ... The room you will have then, or Gauguin if he comes, will have white walls with a decoration of great yellow sunflowers ... you will see these great pictures of sunflowers, 12 or 14 to the bunch, crammed into this tiny boudoir with its pretty bed and everything else dainty. It will not be commonplace."

Here, he's describing his second series of sunflower paintings, created in Arles in 1888 in anticipation of the ill-fated (or infamous) visit from his friend and fellow painter, Paul Gauguin. The overarching motivation appears to have been the creation of a decorative display for the Yellow House.

To mark the 134th anniversary of Vincent van Gogh's death, his sunflowers shall be on show at the National Gallery's Van Gogh: Poets and Lovers exhibition in London. The show will feature two of Vincent's sunflowers of the seven he painted while in Arles; one from the National's permanent collection, the other usually on display at Philadelphia Museum of Art. Given that we know with certainty Vincent's vision for his sunflowers, it's remarkable that they are most often displayed as individual works in galleries. Even more remarkable, then, is that the upcoming show at the National will mark the first time these two paintings have been seen together in the same room since 1889.

The sunflowers have come to symbolise "a gift" given unconditionally from one human to another. It's deeply rewarding to look beyond their decorative appeal and see them in this light.

A scene from the Yellow House—recreated using the original paintings, just as Gauguin would have found them "crammed into this tiny boudoir with its pretty bed and everything else dainty"—would serve as the most enduring tribute to Vincent, honouring the remarkable gift he left to us.

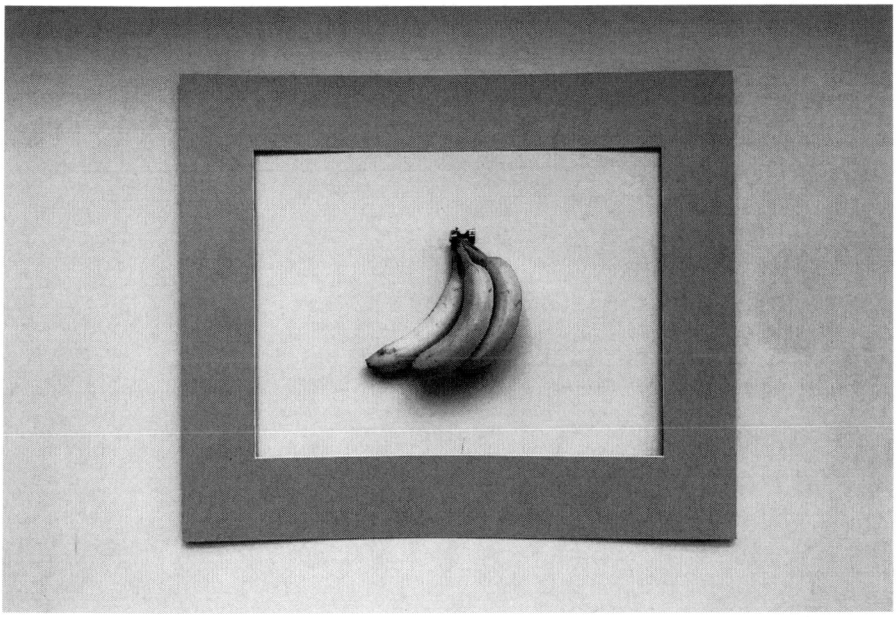

Me, My Banana, My Wall

A Miscreant Ideology of Privileged Hipness

Picasso was ensnared in creation myths, as was Henri Matisse, who also referred to Cezanne as 'the father of us all!' It's true; it's difficult to imagine who else might've breathed life into something equivalent to cubism without Picasso's obsession with the countless images Cezanne made of Mont Sainte-Victoire. But the rise of Modern Art sprang from a diversity of stimuli because it is, of itself, diverse. Paul Cezzane was one of three notable absentees from the discourse around the fashionable salon in Paris at the end of the nineteenth-century: Cezzane in Provence, Vincent van Gogh in Arles, and Paul Gauguin, who left Arles for French Polynesia; all three independently unique and powerful influences amongst a plethora of other radical aesthetes that opened the door to the rise of Modernism a few decades later.

Cubism, Fauvism, Abstract expressionism, Futurism, Surrealism, Pop art, Bauhaus, Conceptual art, Suprematism, Vorticism, Orphism, Social realism: Pablo Picasso was directly responsible for some, indirectly for most. The painter, sculptor, lithographer, engraver, and potter, the protagonist of the twentieth century, was shaped by a media craving brash concepts into a phenomenon dedicated to the proposition that the essence of art is that part which can't be explained, a deconstruction in painting, where all that is deemed unnecessary is reduced.

Would any of those early protagonists countenance the prospect that they'd open a door to something quite so terminal as an *art factory*, or still worse, a fatal pathway to an orthodoxy with no capacity to welcome new radicals and the malady of an infantile belief in the

existence of an avant-garde in the Art of Painting?
Time ravishes and waits for no one. But some things are more ravished than others, and this has come to pass: we advance, not in the wake of the new, but on a broad front reliant on tiny nuances of the old tethered to a miscreant ideology of privileged hipness. But if we were to divert the trajectory ending in such disillusionment, would the outcomes not change? Yes. But still, if artists are demonised because they create art considered unworthy by an establishment grounded in a faux bohemia, then it's clear, those critics love the demon more than the demonised.

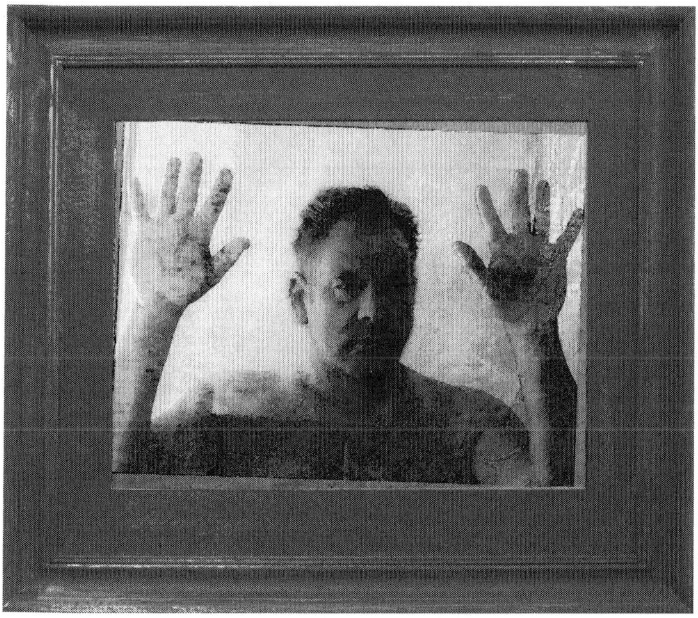

A Gallery Without Walls

The Art of Digital Intelligence

The tumult of war in the twentieth century led to seismic ideological and sociological change, and the onset of our digital world pointed the way to the new order of globalisation. J. Robert Oppenheimer‘s putative phantom of an immutable binary choice, which, once agreed upon, could never be undone, also applied to many other things that changed during that century, only most of those other things were metaphorically less binary than the predetermined act of inventing the atom bomb. We could eulogise about the advent of modernism in art and its coupling with societal evolution, but the pace at which the digital happened made it a revolution, not an evolution, and the visual arts appeared to lack a credible pace-maker within the half-life of the radioactive isotopes decaying on earth since the bomb, to keep up with it.

I first sat and typed at a keyboard in the late seventies. It was a Teleprinter terminal keyboard fitted with a roll of paper with perforated edges so that it could be rolled up on sprockets. A single line of code would be typed, printed on the paper roll, then transmitted over a serial connection for storage and processing. Computer programs were archived on decks of punched cards before reel-to-reel tape made its way into our college. In just a few intervening years—in time of my indoctrination into the world of work—keyboards with Cathode Ray Tube-fired Visual Display Units were integrated into the typical workstation and more manageable forms of magnetic media were used for storing programs and data. There was something tactile about the whirling hum of the ungainly electrical paraphernalia we used back then to develop software. We programmed close to the bare metal when, with limited resources, bits and bytes needed to be counted. And, we worshiped one thing above all else; the oracle locked away from plain sight in its cleanroom citadel: the mainframe computer; a brute-force triumph of engineering ingenuity. The experience was relatively short-lived, as were most things during the revolution: within the first few formative years of a career in computer science, the mass-produced Personal Computer was upon us. Every developer had a dedicated Central Processing Unit at their disposal boxed up inside a system unit sitting neatly on the desk. We knew we were riding the crest of something radical as an elite software engineering community set about building layers of abstractions—software components that isolate the complexities of underlying infrastructures—to help the next generation of superusers to evade some of the devil we all knew to exist lurking in the detail. By the end of the revolution, we'd developed Operating Systems, high-level programming language compilers, Graphical User Interfaces, and we'd wired together our boxes to build local networks hosting distributed systems. We were the new radicals who turned up to work in crumpled shirts reeling in the spirit of non-compliance, raging against the mandatory dress code.

Then came the Internet.

At the beginning, I disparagingly accepted the commodification of photography due to the instantaneousness of digital devices. Instead of cherished memories delicately dodged, burned, developed, and fixed as prints under the safe light of the darkroom, a new model arose—one in which happy snaps swelled the photo hoard to terabyte-sized chunks, stored in an unseen cloud, floating about like unloved relics, as if awaiting their accidental discovery sometime in the future. I was, however, soon convinced that digital technology offered an exciting new and extensible future-proof medium for creatives, albeit antithetical to the centuries of evolved practices applied to the making of art destined for display in physical spaces. Although systems for rendering digital formats into physical forms have found their way into the ubiquity of the art-making workflow—colour printing and scanning, spring to mind—the world is now also served by a plethora of software applications specialising in simulation, image processing, geometry modelling, visualisation, audio, video, animation, gaming; a hybrid of tools supporting the creation of fantastical virtual realities. Applications shrunk into apps and embedded into pocket-sized devices—supercomputers by any standard of an earlier generation—and, thanks to the technological advances in digital signal processing, leverage the huge power of location transparency within the global network to offer a new idiom—a virtual gallery for art—as transformative and immersive in its consumption as it is in its creation.

Computers have always been good for two things: recalling information (memory) and performing tasks (thinking) quickly. An impressive capacity for memory recall and the ability to think fast would undoubtedly be two distinguishing qualities of animal intelligence, but not so of intelligent computers. However, the definition of artificial intelligence (AI) provides a handy clarification in this respect by including *reasoning* and *learning* into the scope of its definition.

The benefits I saw in Expert Systems—the forerunner to AI—back in the early nineteen nineties, considerably predates the fervour on the lips of thought gurus today on the subject of AI. Its lengthy gestation is probably indicative of its growth in lock-step with the volume of data accessible in the public domain commensurate with big data processing techniques and the astonishing rate at which raw computing power has evolved. At its heart, AI is an inference engine—typically deployed as part of the software stack, although increasingly integrated as on-chip systems—that employs domain specific rules and a given data set to evaluate both deterministic and probable outcomes.

Kurt Friedrich Gödel's incompleteness theorems [1931] stipulate that in a formal system, there will always be statements that are true but unprovable by the system, and consequently, that such a system is incapable of demonstrating its own consistency. In other words, Gödel's system can compute according to its known rules, but cannot compute why its rules exist. Furthermore, if a system were to generate its own rules, other statements that are true but unprovable by the new system could be written ad infinitum. The philosopher John Randolph Lucas' *Minds, Machines and Gödel* [1961] and latterly physicist Roger Penrose's *The Emperor's New Mind* [1989], extend the principle and assert that it is impossible to construct a machine based on computational theory that has the same cognitive abilities as humans; conversely, that the human mind is not a machine. In a similar way, the famous Turing Test [Alan Turing] is also designed to evaluate a machine's ability to exhibit human behaviour by having it engage in a natural language conversation and to adjudge, through an observer, which of the two participants in the conversation is human and which is machine. If we consider art, in all its forms, as a language developed by humans to convey the essential nature of what it means to *be* human, and if we subscribe to the Gödelian argument and accept that conciseness is manifested through understanding grounded in human intelligence, then the proposition arises that any synthesis of art created by machines alone shall always fail the Turing test and, therefore, can only ever be fully appreciated by those willing to abandon the essentiality of nature.

The AI paradigm opens the door to controversy in the arts space over the question of material ownership and the imperative of upholding artists' creative rights, and of originality when outcomes are imitative of the given domain. Although to some this may appear disconcerting, the only logical way to confront the singularly pervasive threat of digital representation, is to embrace the idea that the process by which *original* art is created is entirely irrelevant. For those invested in that idea, the liberation offered to them by our current standing in the cycle of technological evolution opens the door to creative freedoms immeasurably more expansive than the protagonists of modernism could've conceivably envisaged over a century ago. For the others, this won't just go away; a seminal CR/LF has already been typed on our collective keyboard that can't be undone as hardware shrinks ever smaller, the world's datastore grows ever bigger, and ever smarter processors continue to shift electrons ever faster.

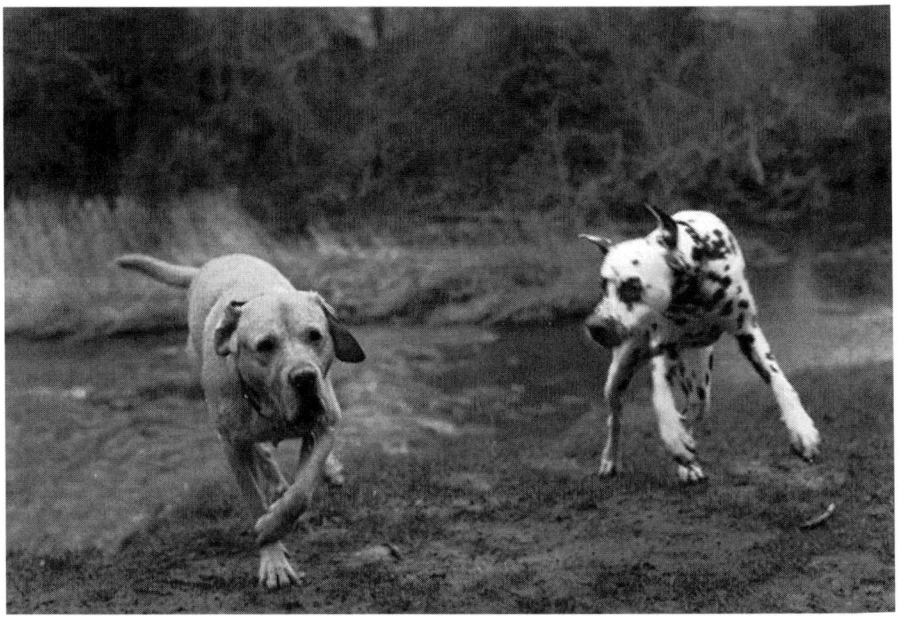

Rivalry

Dog Eats Dog Striving for Perfection

I sat and watched old people scraping up the remains of their gravy—a muscle memory guiding their knives and forks and mouthlike parts. They sensed nothing save the metronome beat till the end of days keeping time with conformity. It seemed like the bright flame needed to outshine the giant had long been extinguished in them. And I pondered: is the urge for competitiveness a learned instinct or innate within us all? Might it be diminished as we grow old? When people yield to their hidden instincts and describe themselves as competitive, I inwardly brace myself against the wrangle of a feigned friendship developing between us. Even making allowances for an excusable brevity of thinking, I'm estranged from the competitive instinct and so immune to the insidiousness of rivalries that potentially shape the influences motivating artists to make art.

History is examined as a continuum flowing like a river from one inflection point to the next—it revels in the here and now then travels hopefully to the next great thing—but there is no logical destination for it, nor is there any certainty that the discrete events acting within it can influence its direction of travel. When events become reactive, tremendous forces of nature can occur, but the farther we reach downstream of them, the less cogent they appear. To restore relics as a force in art, we must look deeper into the murk beneath the surface in search of artists' cultural and personal influences, discover those they imitated as peers, and recognise the motivation that lay in their obsession to surpass them as rivals.

Georgio Vasari frequently refers to 'contests' in his celebrated book of the Italian Renaissance, *The Lives of the Artists*, in which he devotes 75 pages to

Michelangelo, 33 to Rafael, and only 14 to Leonardo da Vinci. If we consider legacy purely in terms of oeuvres left to posterity which endure beyond prejudice in the eyes of those who'd speak out about 'greatness', then as far as that goes, I'd say Vasari has it about right! But, Vasari's narrative, compounded by his pejorative language, is trained within the contemporary normative view of what made so-called good art back in the sixteenth century. The same view was held by benefactors and practitioners alike and this laid the ground rules to be followed by artists competing for recognition. Vasari eulogises about Michelangelo in The Lives,

He [God] decided, in order to rid us of so many errors, to send to earth a spirit who, working alone, was able to demonstrate in every art and every profession the meaning of perfection in the art of design, how to give relief to the details in paintings by means of proper drawing, tracing, shading, and casting light, how to work with good judgement in sculpture, and how to make buildings comfortable and secure, healthy, cheerful, well proportioned, and richly adorned with various decorations in architecture.

From Vasari's treatment, we can extrapolate to some of the norms which, when considered together with the use of religious motifs, reveal how the period of the Italian Renaissance may be delineated from other cultural movements founded in the dream of rebirth. But, importantly, Vasari's discourse also presents a fairly narrow blueprint designed to glorify the clergy's preachings about god and the miraculous lives of the saints in the eyes of a largely illiterate audience, according to which, competitors competed in an organised state of rivalry. But, the blueprint also pivots around Vasari's rhetoric, filled, as it is, with subjective verdicts about artists surpassing one another, and by the idolising of the good and the better. Perhaps Vasari's is a reflection on a period when the primordial force of survival was a naturalistic predilection inherent in classical antiquity founded on conquest, and the ongoing warring enmity between regional states before annexation of the Italian peninsula. On the other hand, there were a great many Madonna's and altarpieces needed to adorn the churches of Rome and Florence! Vasari's own idol, Michelangelo, developed a notable rivalry (according to him) with his elder, Leonardo da Vinci. If imitation is indeed flattery, the twenty three year old Michelangelo certainly imbued the face of his *Pietà* with the striking resemblance to a number of Leonardo's Virgin Marys. But, it was Michelangelo's idealised aesthetic that won the day in their quest to exemplify the epitome of perfection.

A turn in the river doesn't signify an iteration of a state nearing an ideal to be imitated, but a change in the blueprint itself. It's neat and tidy to talk about movements in art as a chronology—we seem to crave such simplicity—where each transition is beyond an event horizon that rejects the pathologies seen to exist in the previous movement. The catholic reaction to the reformation in Rome, transitioned Renaissance art to the Baroque. In 1672 Giovanni Pietro Bellori published a series of biographies of contemporary artists including that of Michelangelo Merisi da Caravaggio (commonly known to us as Caravaggio). He wrote,

"But he [Caravaggio] worked reluctantly at these things and felt deeper regret at not being able to paint figures. When he met Prospero, a painter of grotesques, he took the opportunity to leave Giuseppe in order to compete with him for the glory of painting. Then he began to paint according to his own inclinations; not only ignoring but even despising the

superb statuary of antiquity and the famous paintings of Raphael, he considered nature to be the only subject fit for his brush....Since Caravaggio aspired only to the glory of colour, so that the complexion, skin, blood and natural surfaces might appear real, he directed his eye and work solely to that end, leaving aside all the other aspects of art."

Interestingly, Bellori remarks on the tradition of the contest and Caravaggio's vexatious attitude toward tradition. But, crucially, he is forthright regarding Caravaggio's conviction in putting realism at the centre of his form of expression at the expense of all else that had gone before him. Bellori also writes,

"Therefore, in order to find figure types and to compose them, when he came upon someone in town who pleased him he made no attempt to improve on the creation of nature."

Caravaggio's radical form of naturalism, illuminated under the vivid spotlight of chiaroscuro, had the impactful effect of challenging the sensibilities of his patrons, and in doing so, disrupt both the religious and secular orthodoxy in art. In 1603 the painter and historian Giovanni Baglione prosecuted a legal case against several artists, including Caravaggio, for libellous statements made against him that'd been circulated around Rome. It's alleged that the defamatory verses were written in response to a lucrative commission for an altarpiece Baglione had completed by imitating Caravaggio's style and in which he'd included a caricature of Caravaggio appearing as a grotesque devil. The intense rivalry for church commissions is evident in the acrimonious exchanges documented between the two artists before, during, and long after the legal case that resulted in Caravaggio's imprisonment—this would not be his last misery suffered in prison nor agony at the hands of his enemies.

In 1642 Baglione published his posthumous biography of Caravaggio—Bellori's text is partly derived from Baglione—in which, about Caravaggio's masterpieces at the Contarelli Chapel in san Luigi dei Francesi, he said,

"This commission with the paintings done after life, together with those of Cavaliere Giuseppe, whose talent aroused a certain envy on the part of his colleagues, made Caravaggio famous, and the paintings were excessively praised by evil people."

Baglione is similarly derogatory and dismissive about other works and successes of Caravaggio, but he ends on this note,

"If Michelangelo Merisi had not died so soon, the art world would have profited greatly from his beautiful style, which consisted of painting from nature"

Caravaggio fought fiercely and won his opportunity to change the river's course. In doing so, perhaps he helped propel a current along a strait connecting two entirely separate oceans: in *David with the Head of Goliath*, did Caravaggio urge his audience to wonder at the might of the righteous underdog—as it is allegorically—or are we meant to feel pity in the presence of his tortured self-portrait as he fled as a fugitive made of his own rivalrous instinct?

In the words of Robert de la Sizeranne, published in 1903 in his essay *The Oil Paintings of J.M.W. Turner,*

"With none other is it so hard to differentiate in his art between that which impels one to say, "I have seen that!" and that which causes one to exclaim, "How I should like to see that!" or to discover of what sort is the transformation which operated in his imagination and in his hand, in order that such things might be possible."

The perception of the "transformative" was keenly observed by commentators through the spectre of the Royal Academy of Arts at the time of Turner's election as an Academician in 1802. The arc of Turner's transformation was initially propelled by his resurrection of Claude Loraine's precursor to romanticism at a time when the institution had fostered a critical discourse around the classical ideal of landscape painting in England. John Constable entered the Academy Schools ten years later than Turner and he first exhibited in the same year as Turner's election to RA. Constable's association with the Royal Academy of Arts was slow to start in comparison, and seemingly more problematic. He was certainly no prodigy: elected as an Associate in 1819, and, despite being only one year Turner's junior, he only became an Academician in 1829—at the age of fifty-two—scraping in by an inauspicious single vote. Contrast that, if you will, with Turner, who joined the Academy School at the age of fourteen. So, the scene was set for a less than equitable competition in their much-debated rivalry. So, was it really a case of sparring adversaries: in the red corner, ye olde cockney geezer, and in the blue, the son of a country gentleman? Or is our perception of it today a figment of the commentary surrounding the ideal vision of landscape seen through the prism of an institutionalised Royal Academy in the early nineteenth-century? There's little real evidence of visceral personal animosity exchanged between them during their tenures, rather, flurries of rancour emanating from the hanging committee with artists' advocates contending for prestigious exhibition space, and varnishing day antics theatrically played-out amidst the swelling politics of critical voices debating the true nature of landscape. Might their naturally opposing styles give rise to a helpful parity—a shop window for critical debate—with the title contenders ushered to the fore like champion prizefighters centre stage? To the outside observer, this surely would've had a polarising effect on their respective corners.

For both Turner,

"... that rare species of landscape, which is addressed more directly to the imagination rather than memory, and which places it in the same class of intellect with Poetry."

... and for Constable,

"... approaches near to the actual look of rural nature ... fresh and powerful transcripts from nature are convincing proofs of her superiority to the sophistications of art."

...the debates about poetic idealism—bordering on absurdity—and naturalism—bordering on bucolic—persisted. Turner's increasingly untempered use of colour, his fluid compositions, and his seminal preoccupation with the impact of industrialisation, and Constable's composite splattering of white highlights and the currency of his spectacular full-sized oil sketches, opened the doors to both Impressionism and Modernism. The enduring question of how far Turner's transformation—from the early influence of Claude to his eccentric fishy monsters, and his immersion in the clamour of the Industrial Revolution—was shaped not only by his empathetic response to its social consequences but also by the rivalries and critical discourse attracted by the Academy during his lifelong alliance with such a prestigiously influential institution.

If jealousy refuses to acknowledge good in the endeavours of rivals, then acclaim must flow through the establishment that owns the blueprint. Thankfully, this is now more equitably divested into the care of the human collective. It's still the same river, the same rate of flow, even if its energy appears suppressed beneath its calm; it just runs broader and ever more shallow when a great multitude of nuance defuses the contentiousness brought about by competition.

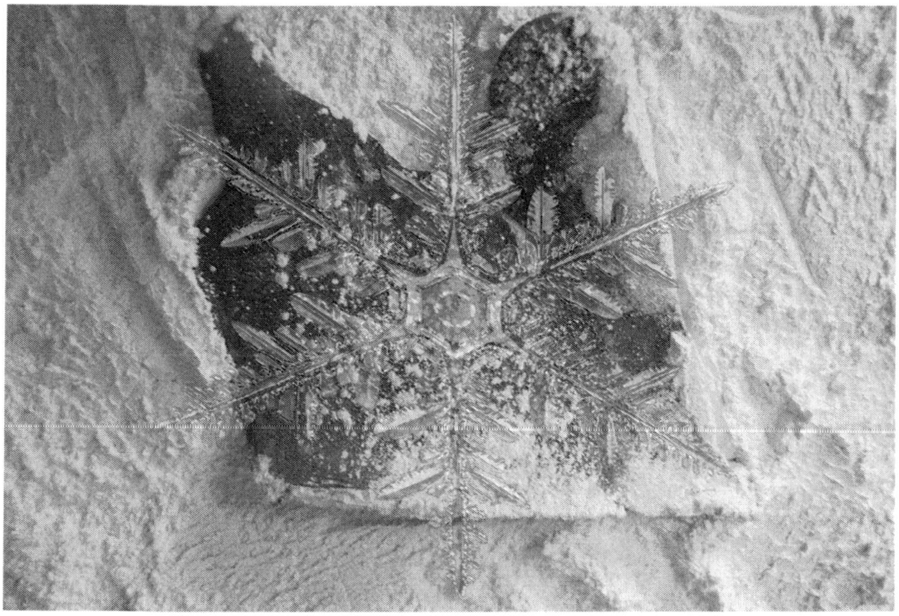

The Terrible Magic of Flake White

Snow Isn't Just Frozen Rain

Unlike frozen water, snowflakes are composed of ice crystals that grow in clouds when water vapour condenses and is frozen directly without becoming liquid water. Ice can grow with a number of different molecular lattices, but the range of conditions found in the earths atmosphere coupled with the fundamental shape of the water molecule, generally forces ice molecules to form into a hexagonal ring with an oxygen atom at each of its six vertices and hydrogen bonds as its edges. The crystalline structures of snowflakes grow following their underlying hexagonal lattice, but the patterns formed within them are beautifully unique, reflecting the chaotic weather systems within which they grow. Johannes Kepler keenly observes the fascinating symmetry found in ice crystals in his essay *The Six-Cornered Snowflake*. The myriad of minute, obliquely oriented facets within a snowflake's fragile crystalline lattice reflect and refract light, causing all visible wavelengths to be emitted equally. This phenomenon, known as *scattering*, is largely the reason why snow appears white. Other optical effects can be attributed to the same phenomenon. For example, when sunlight interacts with air molecules smaller than its wavelength, a kind of scattering occurs—known as Rayleigh scattering—which causes light of shorter wavelengths (at the blue end of the visible spectrum) to scatter more effectively. One of the earliest explanations of this phenomenon came from Leonardo da Vinci himself, who postulated that it is not the air, but rather the particles suspended within it, that give the sky its blue colour.

Kepler's New Year's gift reminds us of the visceral charm of winter, when our rainbow everyday is shrouded in a coat of snow, and the affection for our loved vistas is cancelled beneath the unfamiliar wonderland of its brilliant whiteness. Winter's snow reappears dutifully as a compelling backdrop to artistic themes throughout the history of painting: the bitter confection of L. S. Lowry and the theatre of Pieter Bruegel reinforce icy hardship through stark contrasts of light and dark and, where narrative tightens its winter grip, epics like John Waterhouse's *St. Eulalia* summon the deathly cold to evoke the pathos of the romantic tragedy.

Notwithstanding the obvious fact that white objects are painted white, the bulk of pigment contained within the fine layers of a painting is also likely to be white, especially when paint is applied opaquely. Artists' suppliers would attest that white paint is generally sold in larger volumes than any other colour. In most cases, white serves primarily to soften the intensity of saturated hues. A common device for such "tinting" can be seen in landscape painting, where the saturation of colours is adjusted according to the perceived distance of objects from the viewer, in a technique known as atmospheric perspective. A close inspection of the corpus of our most treasured masterpieces reveals a particular kind of white: Flake White (historically known as Lead White)—a pigment whose optical and rheological properties are of immense importance when studying the history of oil painting techniques and their implications in modern practice. The scattering effects within the crystalline lattice of Flake White plays a fundamental role in hue, opacity, and tinting strength performance. And when combined with a judicious use of binding medium in paint preparation, its elasticity and viscosity can be controlled significantly to enhance the paint's tactile quality, influencing its levelling properties that can be adjusted for both impasto and thin layers of brilliant white imprimatura.

Nicolas Flamel was said to have discovered the highest achievement in alchemy: the transmutation of a base metal into gold—otherwise known as the Philosopher's Stone. To the medieval alchemist, engaged in discovery through practice, experiment, and observation, yet without the privileged understanding of modern science, the alloying of zinc with copper into brass, which in many respects resembles gold, could easily have been interpreted as a transcendental act. In reality, alchemy was nothing more than the early flourishing of chemistry. Similar to a method described by Pliny [AD23/24-79] in *Natural History*, the making of the whitest pigment known to artists, might well have been lauded as a mystical alchemical experiment, transforming lead into a metaphorical gold: 'suspend lead (refined from galena) over vinegar in a container buried alongside horse or cow dung. Vapours of acetic acid released from the vinegar react with the lead, forming lead acetate. Meanwhile, carbon dioxide released from the decomposing manure—which also provides an important source of heat—dissolves in moisture to form carbonic acid gas, which then reacts with the lead acetate to convert the corroded metal into flakes of basic lead carbonate.' The method was developed on an industrial scale by stacking layers of earthenware pots filled with coiled lead strips suspended above vinegar pools, each pot then covered with manure. The technique is still referred to as the "stack process" or the "Old Dutch method." Various modern adaptations of this method for producing Flake White were developed primarily to eliminate the need for animal faeces while preserving the essential chemistry of the process.

Historical records reveal that Leonardo da Vinci purchased different grades of lead white pigment for use in his work. Similar bills of materials, along with technical analyses of numerous other historic paintings (and samples)—from Renaissance Italy to the Dutch Golden Age—indicate a common practice of combining lead white with calcite (a naturally occurring form of calcium carbonate, mainly chalk) in varying proportions, often within the upper layers of a single painting. In such cases, whether modifications to basic, dry lead white pigment—such as the addition of chalk—were motivated by economy; whether higher grades of lead white involved additional post-production refinement; and whether these variations were offered by artists' suppliers or adjusted in the studio, is difficult to ascertain. It is known, however, that multiple washings or reprecipitation steps were used during the Renaissance to purify or brighten lead white, and vinegar could be employed again during these stages to help dissolve impurities. This, along with further fine grinding, may account for the availability of different grades of dry product. We might even venture to suggest that Leonardo da Vinci deliberately employed lead white with sufficiently small crystallite dimensions to promote a bluish tint in specific passages of paint as a direct consequence of his observation of the phenomena of Rayleigh scattering. Whatever the motivation, it is unquestionable that lead white—used in various grades and compounds—formed the basis of the only viable white paint available to artists until the end of the eighteenth century. The legacy of this single source of material in western culture is legendary: Leonardo da Vinci (High Renaissance, Italy), Titian (Venetian Renaissance, Italy), Hans Holbein the Younger (Northern Renaissance, Germany/England), Caravaggio (Early Baroque, Italy), Peter Paul Rubens (Flemish Baroque, Flanders/ Belgium), Nicolas Poussin (French Baroque, France), Diego Velázquez (Spanish Baroque, Spain), Rembrandt van Rijn (Dutch Golden Age, Netherlands), Francisco Goya (Romanticism, Spain), Jacques-Louis David (Neoclassicism, France), J.M.W. Turner (Romanticism, England).

So why is such demonstrable magic so terrible? All lead compounds—including lead acetate, known as sweet "sugar of lead"—are highly toxic. In artists' pigments like Flake White, the greatest health risk arises from inhaling lead particles (dust) or ingesting other materials contaminated with lead compounds. Accordingly, following guidance from various regulatory authorities, the supply of Flake White is now heavily restricted in both the European Union and the United Kingdom. The manufacture of general-purpose paints containing lead is prohibited, while lead-based pigments for artists' use are permitted only under strict conditions—typically reserved for use by conservators. Although Zinc White (known as a compound since antiquity, but first proposed as a pigment in 1782) offered an alternative, Flake White remained the predominant choice on artists' palettes (alongside Zinc) due to its opacity and superior modelling properties like its "ropiness" and '"long body" characteristics. Interestingly, Titanium White (discovered in 1791) was not introduced commercially until the early 20th century—presumably as a non-toxic replacement for Flake White in popular tube-form—but, this also differs to Flake White in various aspects of its use. Naturally, both newer pigments possess optical and rheological properties that would've been unfamiliar to the aforementioned masters, who were accustomed to mulling flakes of lead—with or without supplements—optimised to their accustomed school of practice using in-house specially formulated binding mediums, also adjusted depending on the various demands of optical and rheological requirements, as well as economy. I would argue that the composition of white pigments most profoundly influences overall aesthetic outcomes more than any other: fundamentally, the degree of light scattering depends on particle size and shape, along with the refractive index of the dried binder, while surface effects are governed by the paint's viscous and elastic moduli, which in turn are determined by the pigment's molecular composition and the pigment-to-binder ratio. In both respects, it's impossible to discount the effects of the binding medium, where inestimable subtleties are hidden within its properties. The speculation surrounding the composition of Rembrandt's binding medium is testament to this fact, with suggested recipes ranging from exotic tree resins to mayonnaise.

Taking the three candidates for dry white pigment, namely Zinc White, Titanium White, and Flake White—each mixed with an equal volume of binding medium and selected coloured pigments: they consistently rank in that order with respect to tinting strength—the ability to lighten and desaturate the mixture—however, this is considerably influenced by the significant disparity in particle size and its consequential effect on light scattering in the mixture. The same order applies when considering increasing density, particle size, and viscosity, with Flake White producing a more malleable and hefted mixture under the palette knife—of the other two, Titanium White is much closer to Flake White on these measures.

Recognising such a complex and subtle array of properties, and then also to consider other factors like cost and convenience, represents a multi-criteria optimisation problem, where more than one objective must be optimised simultaneously. This challenge implies, as Leonardo da Vinci was aware, that the same formula for white paint is not needed, nor indeed desirable, for everything—one size does not fit all! Even setting cost and convenience aside, the challenge of combining optical and rheological properties to meet a specific application remains a complex optimisation problem. Artists may not need to be acutely aware of underlying chemistry and physics: the role of lead in Flake White as a drying accelerant through its catalytic effect on oil oxidation; how light scattering is induced by particle size and the differences in refractive index between the pigment and its binder, thus affecting tinting strength and the luminosity of glazes. But, much like the intricate distinctiveness of individual snowflakes, the nature of such hidden variables all contribute to the greater challenge: mastering the behaviour of light using nothing but paint. For myself, navigating the multi-criteria optimisation problem is, in many ways, part of the joy of painting itself!

In a contemporary context, the hope that white paint taken from the same tube can perform and adapt to meet all expectations relies on a blind faith in its scientifically formulated universality. It's also almost certain that the basic pigment relied upon for the colour white now differs significantly from that used for centuries. In the world of Leonardo da Vinci, such a resulting lack of nuance would certainly have been considered a very discerning compromise.

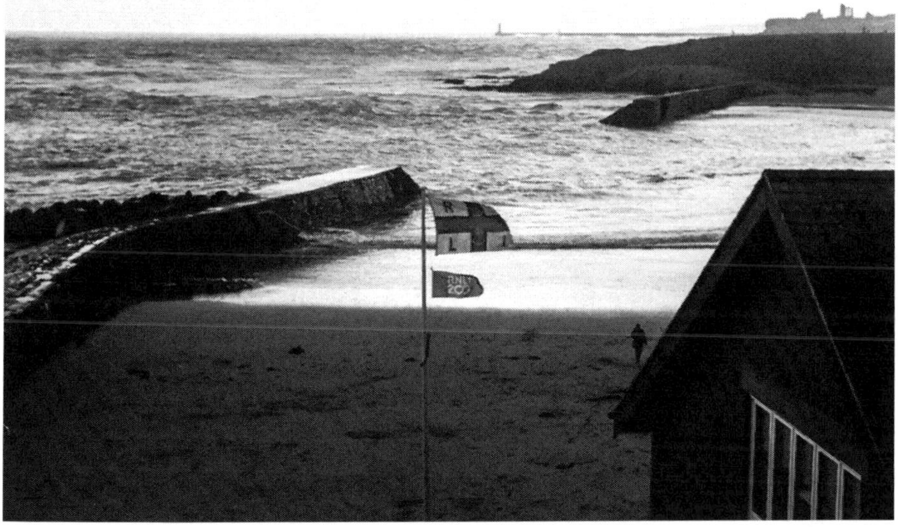

Born in America. Made in Cullercoats

Winslow Homer

There is little doubt that the development of early industry flourished along the River Tyne due to the abundance of coal which could be found in relatively shallow seams down to the shore. It was over one hundred years before Howdon Pans gave up its salt when a traveller landed at the river stairs, wrote: "each pan makes one tun and a quarter of salt at eight boilings, which lasts three days and a half. Each consumes fourteen chaldrons of coals in seven days; in which time it makes two tuns and a half of salt." A glass-making firm had been established by a family of French nobles; its clay ovens raged in the familiar heat of coal, melting sand, and the village population grew not unused to the miracle of it; digging fathoms deeper for it, and the industry of transporting it, freshly hewn, along mile-upon-mile of wagon-ways from pits sank farther afield, down to boats and keels waiting on the river. Along the slither of Willington Gut, beneath the splendour of the viaduct arches, ran a ropery. Its distant forebears had taken a foothold in this place at a time when hemp rope was in eager demand for the making and mending of stays, shrouds, sheets, and halyards, of the seventy or so wooden vessels built at Capt. Francis Hurry's shipbuilding yard at Howdon Pans. The yard was established forty years before Lord Nelson's famous victory over the French at Cape Trafalgar and grew to a formidable scale compared to any other contemporary merchant builder: four slipways, a double graving dock, sailmaking and moulding loft and the ropery, and a quay occupying eight hundred feet or so of river frontage, rose as a pre-eminent force rivalling anything in England. With the abundance of coal commensurate with the volumes needed to smelt iron and fire steam engines mounted on keels, at the home of the 'father of railways', George Stephenson, and birthplace of his son, Robert, workers turned full-tilt against the cleft, and moulded their renewed lives around the challenge of constructing iron ships. By the mid-nineteenth century, the streets along the Tyne lay crowded with scant accommodation for the mass influx of metal workers as shipbuilding transformed. But, as the 'new order' brought new willing hands, the disorder of overcrowding amidst the clamour for industrialisation, inflicted a life of poverty upon most toiling within those communities.

The fleet of colliers busying at the Northumberland Dock grew unabated as land was recovered along the foreshore using the ballast material now taken directly from vessels to raise the ground to a healthy level. Old tenements situated near the riverside were demolished; Captain Hurry's house near the old dock yard and George Stephenson's cottage were also stricken, and a great deal more at the former hot-bed of cholera; all buried under ballast as the foundation for the promise of spacious streets forty feet wide. The Whittle Dean Water Company laid their pipes carrying clean water from Fontburn Reservoir. A gas making plant illuminated twelve street lamps at the old Howdon village, and the haunted walls of the Willington flour mill turned its head to steam, and to the west, capital works for the manufacture of iron arrived to meet the new order: blast furnaces constructed, mighty beam engines of a scale previously unseen, and steam boilers worked cranes at the Killingworth Drops took vessels of over two-hundred feet in length into deep water berths sufficient for ships of eight-hundred tons north of Cockcrow Sands. The block and mast maker, the caulker, the iron moulder, the iron ship rivet heater, the riveter, the pattern maker, the dock labourer, the boilersmith, did all they knew and knew well: they plied their trades, in toil, sweat, and blood.

I moved up the road from my birthplace at Howdon to the coast north of the Port of Tyne in 1985. I lived within a literal stone's throw away from the Watch House that overlooks the beach at Cullercoats Bay. There's no evidence supporting why the American painter Winslow Homer came there and then decided to stay for almost two years. He spent the first three months during his trip to England from March 1881 in London. He would've visited the Royal Academy—they all did—and witnessed at first hand the legacy that J. M. W. Turner left to his generation—he may even perhaps heard tell of the highly prized Wallsend coals arriving at the London Docks.

When in the North East, he undoubtedly would've ridden the Riverside Line over the viaduct arches at Willington Quay shrouded in its veil of black smoke and coal dust, its vistas jarred by the harsh reality of the Industrial Revolution that consumed the region then; of shipbuilding, mining for coal, and the railways. Turner had also travelled along the River Tyne [*The Hurries, Coal Boats Loading, North Shields; Keelmen Heaving in Coals by Moonlight; Tynemouth, from North Shields; The High Light North Shields, Tynemouth Priory*], feverishly recording the brutal impact of industrialisation on the British landscape in his watercolours. This became Turner's seminal preoccupation. But, Homer, the straw-boater'd, tweed-suite'd, white-collar'd, elegant, quiet American, stumbled upon a different kind of nature when he fetched up at the Hudleston Arms Hotel and watched a die-hard band of locals mending their nets and cobles at Cullerçoats: the nature endured by fisherfolk in their perilous struggle for survival on the sea, united in the fellowship of their community.

Perhaps Homer did glimpse the sandy coast ravished by the North Sea in Turner's pictures at the Royal Academy in London, or heard of the river famed for its maritime industry, of Wallsend coals, or of Lord Collingwood and his Tars of the Tyne watching over the Tynemouth Bar, or of the regions ecclesiastical fame and the godly stature of the Venerable Bede at Tynemouth Priory, or of the ancient Kings of Northumbria. Perhaps some or all of those things drove his curiosity northward, but Cullercoats was no village idyl—still tenuously attached to the hellishness of the coal trade—its little beach, nestled like a haven at the edge of an industrial maelstrom.

Homer's watercolour drawings depicting the fisherfolk (mainly younger fisherwomen) at Cullercoats commanded critical acclaim when received in America, and some commentators suggest they mark a turning point in his approach to painting. The stylistic similarity in Homer's manner in these pictures can be seen in the work of Jean-François Millet, whose depiction of peasant folk 'working the fields' to express the dignity of labour through social engagement, is regarded as a key subject in the development of Modernism in Europe. Homer spent time in France between 1866 and 1867—a precursor to his earlier paintings in which he too applied a similar theme to rural life. If Homer had indeed taken inspiration from the 'new modernism', he'd be in good company: a wide diversity of avant-garde artists appearing in the late nineteenth century had similar connections with Millet, when, according to some, he became the best-known modern artist in the world. The interesting point to the Cullercoats story is that the fisherfolk community existed geographically and socially at the edge of a rapidly developing industrial modernity incongruous to their ethereal custom of harvesting the fruits of the sea, and this threatened their very way of life. Their flat-bottomed coble boats, rigged in handsome Dipping Lug sails, were designed for launching from the beach into heady surf and landing in the swell of the North Sea, at a time when the North Shields fishing fleet worked steam powered trawlers and drifters from the shelter of the river. This point may either be a mere adjunct to the story or the key tenet of it; there is very little documented evidence regarding Homer's associations with other artists when he was in residency at Cullercoats, therefore we can't know his exact motivations; his watercolour drawings made during the period remain the only real surviving testament as to why he came there and then decided to stay a while.

Still, I walk the beach at Cullercoats Bay; I see no cobles on the sand nor a halo of gulls hovering in chorus above fisherfolk laden beneath their bountiful creels.

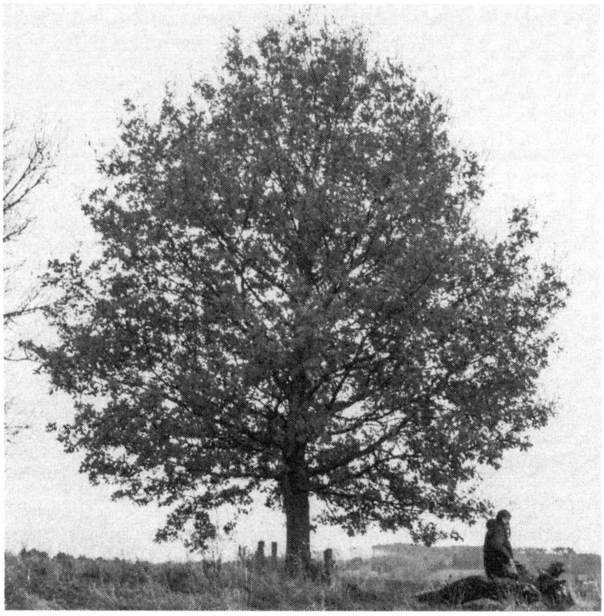

The Iterative Lifecycle Everyday

Shipbuilding and Nature's Creative Workflow

Imagine a spiral with spokes radiating outward from its centre where the spiral represents a system and each of its spokes represents a key artefact of that system—a feature, or function, perhaps. As we're drawn into the vortex of the spiral in a swirling journey towards its centre and complete a full cycle, we encounter each artefact, one by one—the same features, or functions at each iteration—such that, at each encounter, we can evaluate the relative impact to the overall system as a consequence of refinements to its set of artefacts. In such a way, the journey along the spiral's path naturally converges onto an optimal system—within the boundaries of its target requirements—and, allows the observation of changes to a given artefact along the vector of its spoke towards the centre of the spiral. Although the geometric appearance of a spiral may appear abstract in the context of some problem spaces—especially creative ones—the visualisation of a vortex where an increase in order is induced towards its centre—rather like gravity—offers a useful conceptualisation to many problems, especially where cause and effect is not so obvious at the outset.

I slid down Davy Bank in the snow of 1982 on my way to a job interview with the British Ship Research Association. I have at least four generations of shipbuilders on both sides of my family tree, but my version of destiny wasn't inevitable; like the black sheep, I'd just graduated with a degree, so I wasn't inclined to endure the factory lathe any longer nor spend my life welding steel plate. Nothing could have been further removed from the impression I'd been given of the shipbuilding industry than what I'd learn in the few years following those furtive steps through the doors of the Pametrada building, as I arrived dutifully for work on my first day as Research Officer. In those earliest days, I was introduced to the concept of iterative processes—specifically, as applied to the design development of ships. This was presented to me in a paper written in an era before computer-aided optimisation systems were even conceived, let alone implemented. Suffice to say, it described the ship design process unfolding through multiple revolutions around its conceptual spiral, similar to that described above. At the outer iterations, the broader concepts of topology or overall geometry are derived from overarching functional, operational, and financial requirements; preliminary design phases establish scantlings—structural dimensions—while localised elements are largely shaped by fabrication methods and production constraints. Each cycle offers scope for optimisation and compromise within the context of manoeuvrability, seakeeping, resistance and propulsion, and basic trim and stability—considerations that hark all the way back to the ancient Greek mathematician Archimedes—and to the enduring imperative of safeguarding life at sea. Naval architecture, in this sense, is the archetypal balancing act: the art of blending complex structural, functional, and non-functional demands. It draws upon a remarkable range of sciences and disciplines to converge to optimal outcomes. Few pursuits require such multifaceted compromise—and fewer still are as intellectually and creatively compelling. My days spent at the research station at the bottom of Davy Bank enabled me to look back at our ancestors stretching back to the Bronze Age—those who'd set upon the sea, made untamed and cruel by the gravity of the moon—in the spirit of enterprise and hubris, in ships crafted to withstand the unsparing challenges of nature. From wood to steel, from the rivet to the weld, they'd mastered the art of building ships in surprisingly crude and rudimentary conditions. Paradoxically, these remarkable people, conjuring remarkable feats of engineering, produced structures that ranked among the most technically advanced of their time—beautiful forms brought to life through ingenuity, reliant on the most sophisticated applied sciences of their era, and emblematic of national pride and technological progress.

Spirals are often visualised as planar curves—although space curves or helices can be derived as three-dimensional forms—in which, for any point on the curve, the radius (distance from its centre) and the angle (rotation of its radius about the centre) share a mathematical relationship such that the radius increases as the angle increases. Various mathematical relationships give rise to classical spiral topologies, resulting in their distinctive appearances: Lituus, Hyperbolic, Parabolic, and Logarithmic, but perhaps most poignantly, the Archimedean spiral is the best known—where the distance between successive turns is constant such that the spiral grows linearly, maintaining an equal distance between its turns. Even more poignantly perhaps, determining the smoothness of a curve has long been a noble preoccupation in the shipbuilding industry. It was once common practice to make drawings of sections, buttocks, and waterline curves in three primary orthogonal planes—used to define the shape of the hullform in three dimensions (the ship's lines) set out initially on the drawing board—then scaled to full or near full size, marked out on a floorspace usually located in the 'loft' area of a shipyard building. A physical spline—a long, narrow strip of wood—was used to fit curves through specific points, shaped and held in place by heavy weights known as 'ducks'. By adjusting the number and position of ducks, the spline could be made to pass through the required points so that the resulting curve appeared smooth, or 'fair'. This process relied on the natural elasticity of the spline material to produce a catenary between the fixed points. Wooden templates would then be manufactured as a precise fit to the lines on the loft floor and taken to the shipyard's sheds to assist in the fabrication and assembly process.

Process models adopting an iterative lifecycle are applied across many branches of engineering: in the design and development of complex artefacts, and in software development, where they are now universally accepted—having replaced outdated 'big bang' approaches in the interest of reducing cost-related risk. These models are conceptually similar to the foundational principles of Charles Darwin's theory of biological evolution through natural selection, in that convergence onto an optimal outcome is guided by a process of inspection and adaptation applied over successive iterations. Darwin's theory transformed scientific understanding by explaining how species adapt and change over time in response to their environments. His work challenged established beliefs, reshaped biological research, and laid the foundation for modern evolutionary biology, fundamentally transforming how scientists study the natural world and its complex processes. The history of life on Earth seems to indicate that living organisms evolve into more advanced species; evolution increases order, as does convergence onto optimal outcomes. It occurs continuously, and we can be reminded of it, if we look closer, in our everyday lives. Take, for example, a tree: beneath its canopy, there exists a thriving ecosystem—a living environment, a community, a home—sustaining countless species of woodland creatures, insects, and fungi through a complex, cyclical rhythm that repeats every year during a lifespan that can stretch to centuries. Colonies of microscopic insects flourish on its branches, which reach out toward the wind to disperse pollen between flowers, and toward the light, and down into the earth through roots that absorb vital nutrients from the soil. And when an oak is attacked by colonies of microscopic insects—such as the acorn weevil, which burrows deep into swelling acorns; the larvae of the winter moth, which infest the tree to gorge on its young, vulnerable leaves; or the gall wasp laying its eggs—the tree responds through highly organised internal processes. It uses chemicals and hormonal signaling to regulate its internal defense responses while continuing to play a vital role in sustaining life on Earth. It absorbs visible light (via chlorophyll in chloroplasts), carbon dioxide (through stomata), and water (through its roots), converting them into chemical energy through the process of photosynthesis, which produces oxygen and glucose to nourish its growth.

Spirals appear as a recurring motif in nature—seashells, the arrangement of sunflower seeds, and the sweeping arms of distant galaxies. They echo symmetry, balance, and a direction towards increased order in nature. Conceptually, they are unconstrained: they have no boundaries, their centre represents infinity; perhaps they continue to evolve towards an unreachable masterpiece of perfection. In art, the inspiration needed to elicit an emotional human response can arise spontaneously, but the transformation of an idea into a tangible art form often requires a workflow that is fundamentally iterative. This is not, of course, meant to disparage art created entirely in the free spirit of spontaneity;

however, an instrument—whether a keyboard, parchment, canvas, or even a thought experiment—placed in the hands of Beethoven, Shakespeare, or Leonardo da Vinci would unlikely result in a masterpiece without the influence of previous iterations of the same thing.

SPRING 2025

AN ART SCIENTIFIC
PRODUCTION

Printed in Dunstable, United Kingdom

72249595R00032